GOVERNMENT PROCEDURES AND OPERATIONS

AF837132

FEDERAL GRANTS TO STATE AND LOCAL GOVERNMENTS

HISTORICAL PERSPECTIVE AND SELECT CHALLENGES

GOVERNMENT PROCEDURES AND OPERATIONS

Additional books in this series can be found on Nova's website under the Series tab.

Additional E-books in this series can be found on Nova's website under the E-book tab.

GOVERNMENT PROCEDURES AND OPERATIONS

FEDERAL GRANTS TO STATE AND LOCAL GOVERNMENTS

HISTORICAL PERSPECTIVE AND SELECT CHALLENGES

ANDREW E. FISHER
EDITOR

NOVINKA

New York

Copyright © 2013 by Nova Science Publishers, Inc.

All rights reserved. No part of this book may be reproduced, stored in a retrieval system or transmitted in any form or by any means: electronic, electrostatic, magnetic, tape, mechanical photocopying, recording or otherwise without the written permission of the Publisher.

For permission to use material from this book please contact us:
Telephone 631-231-7269; Fax 631-231-8175
Web Site: http://www.novapublishers.com

NOTICE TO THE READER

The Publisher has taken reasonable care in the preparation of this book, but makes no expressed or implied warranty of any kind and assumes no responsibility for any errors or omissions. No liability is assumed for incidental or consequential damages in connection with or arising out of information contained in this book. The Publisher shall not be liable for any special, consequential, or exemplary damages resulting, in whole or in part, from the readers' use of, or reliance upon, this material. Any parts of this book based on government reports are so indicated and copyright is claimed for those parts to the extent applicable to compilations of such works.

Independent verification should be sought for any data, advice or recommendations contained in this book. In addition, no responsibility is assumed by the publisher for any injury and/or damage to persons or property arising from any methods, products, instructions, ideas or otherwise contained in this publication.

This publication is designed to provide accurate and authoritative information with regard to the subject matter covered herein. It is sold with the clear understanding that the Publisher is not engaged in rendering legal or any other professional services. If legal or any other expert assistance is required, the services of a competent person should be sought. FROM A DECLARATION OF PARTICIPANTS JOINTLY ADOPTED BY A COMMITTEE OF THE AMERICAN BAR ASSOCIATION AND A COMMITTEE OF PUBLISHERS.

Additional color graphics may be available in the e-book version of this book.

Library of Congress Cataloging-in-Publication Data

ISBN: 978-1-62417-293-9

Published by Nova Science Publishers, Inc. † New York

CONTENTS

PREFACE

Grants are a form of federal assistance consisting of payments in cash or in kind for a specified purpose and they represent an important tool for achieving national objectives. They vary greatly, including in the types of programs they fund, the methods they use to allocate funds to recipients, and the amount of discretion they give to the grant recipient on how the funds are spent. The Office of Management and Budget (OMB) has previously estimated that grants to state and local governments represent roughly 80 percent of all federal grand funding, with the balance going to recipients such as nonprofit organizations, research institutions, or individuals. This book provides an overview of federal funding levels in a time of fiscal constraint, with a focus on the challenge of continuing to support the current scope and breadth of federal grants to state and local governments.

Chapter 1 – Grants are a form of federal assistance consisting of payments in cash or in kind for a specified purpose and they represent an important tool for achieving national objectives. They vary greatly, including in the types of programs they fund, the methods they use to allocate funds to recipients, and the amount of discretion they give to the grant recipient on how the funds are spent.

The Office of Management and Budget (OMB) has previously estimated that grants to state and local governments represent roughly 80 percent of all federal grant funding, with the balance going to recipients such as nonprofit organizations, research institutions, or individuals. In a time of fiscal constraint, continuing to support the current scope and breadth of federal grants to state and local governments will be a challenge.

In response to a request, this report

1. provides information regarding the amount of grant funding to state and local governments for fiscal year 2011, how such funding has changed over the last three decades, and difficulties related to identifying the exact number of such grant programs; and
2. identifies selected grants management challenges that have been identified in previous work by GAO and federal IGs over the last several years. Towards this end, GAO analyzed data from OMB and the Catalog of Federal Domestic Assistance and conducted a review of previous reports from GAO and federal IGs.

Chapter 2 - The federal government is expected to provide state and local governments more than $612 billion in federal grant-in-aid funding in FY2012, encompassing a wide range of public policies, such as health care, transportation, income security, education, job training, social services, community development, and environmental protection. The central role of federal grants-in-aid in American domestic policy was demonstrated by the prominent role grants-in-aid had in the American Recovery and Reinvestment Act of 2009 (ARRA; P.L. 111-5). ARRA is expected to provide state and local governments about $300 billion in federal grants through 2019.

Congress has a central role in determining the scope and nature of federal grant-in-aid programs. In its legislative capacity, Congress first determines what it wants to accomplish and then decides whether a grant-in-aid program is the best means to achieve it. Congress then selects which of the six grant mechanisms to use (project categorical grant, formula categorical grant, formula-project categorical grant, open-end reimbursement categorical grant, block grant, or general revenue sharing), and crafts legislation to accomplish its purpose, incorporating the chosen grant instrument. As with all legislated programs generally, Congress oversees the program's implementation to ensure that the federal administrating agency is held accountable for making certain that congressional expectations concerning program performance are met.

Federalism scholars agree that congressional decisions concerning the scope and nature of federal grant-in-aid programs are influenced by both internal and external factors. Internal factors include congressional party leadership and congressional procedures; the decentralized nature of the committee system; the backgrounds, personalities, and ideological preferences of individual Members; and the customs and traditions (norms) that govern congressional behavior. Major external factors include input provided by voter constituencies, organized interest groups, the President, and executive branch officials. Although not directly involved in the legislative process, the Supreme Court, through its rulings on federalism issues, also influences congressional decisions concerning federal grant-in-aid programs.

Overarching all of these factors is the evolving nature of cultural norms and expectations concerning government's role in American society. Over time, the American public has become increasingly accepting of government activism in domestic affairs generally, and of federal government activism in particular. Federalism scholars attribute this increased acceptance of, and sometimes demand for, government action as a reaction to the industrialization and urbanization of American society, technological innovations in communications which have raised awareness of societal problems, and exponential growth in economic interdependencies brought about by an increasingly global economy.

This report provides an historical synopsis of the evolving nature of federal grant-in-aid programs, focusing on the role Congress has played in defining the scope and nature of those programs. It begins with an overview of contemporary federal grant-in-aid programs and then examines their evolution over time, focusing on the internal and external factors that have influenced congressional decisions concerning federal grant-in-aid programs. It concludes with an assessment of the scope and nature of the contemporary federal grants-in-aid system and raises several issues for congressional consideration, including possible ways to augment congressional capacity to provide effective oversight of this system.

In: Federal Grants to State and Local Governments ISBN: 978-1-62417-293-9
Editor: Andrew E. Fisher © 2013 Nova Science Publishers, Inc.

Chapter 1

GRANTS TO STATE AND LOCAL GOVERNMENTS: AN OVERVIEW OF FEDERAL FUNDING LEVELS AND SELECTED CHALLENGES*

United States Government Accountability Office

WHY GAO DID THIS STUDY

Grants are a form of federal assistance consisting of payments in cash or in kind for a specified purpose and they represent an important tool for achieving national objectives. They vary greatly, including in the types of programs they fund, the methods they use to allocate funds to recipients, and the amount of discretion they give to the grant recipient on how the funds are spent. The Office of Management and Budget (OMB) has previously estimated that grants to state and local governments represent roughly 80 percent of all federal grant funding, with the balance going to recipients such as nonprofit organizations, research institutions, or individuals. In a time of fiscal constraint, continuing to support the current scope and breadth of federal grants to state and local governments will be a challenge.

In response to a request, this report

* This is an edited, reformatted and augmented version of United States Government Accountability Office, Publication No. GAO-12-1016, dated September 2012.

3. provides information regarding the amount of grant funding to state and local governments for fiscal year 2011, how such funding has changed over the last three decades, and difficulties related to identifying the exact number of such grant programs; and
4. identifies selected grants management challenges that have been identified in previous work by GAO and federal IGs over the last several years. Towards this end, GAO analyzed data from OMB and the Catalog of Federal Domestic Assistance and conducted a review of previous reports from GAO and federal IGs.

What GAO Recommends

GAO is not making any recommendations in this report.

What GAO Found

Federal outlays for grants to state and local governments totaled more than $606 billion in fiscal year 2011. Over the last three decades, these grants have consistently been a significant component of federal spending, but the focus of this spending has changed over time. For example, during this period the proportion of federal outlays to state and local governments dedicated to Medicaid grants more than tripled, rising from 2.4 percent of total federal government outlays in 1980 to 7.6 percent in 2011. The increase in federal outlays for Medicaid and other health-related grant programs was offset by an approximately equivalent decrease in grants to state and local governments targeted for other areas such as transportation, education, and regional development.

GAO's prior work and the work of others have also shown that the number of federal grant programs directed to state and local governments has generally increased over the last three decades. However, definitively determining the number of such grant programs presents difficulties. The lack of consensus on a methodology for how to define and count grant programs and data limitations in the Catalog of Federal Domestic Assistance further complicates this effort.

GAO and federal inspectors general (IG) have previously reported on a variety of management challenges involving federal grants to state and local governments, many of which can be grouped into the following five topic areas:

- **Challenges related to effectively measuring grant performance:** A lack of appropriate performance measures and accurate data can limit agencies' ability to effectively measure grant program performance. This can affect the ability of federal agencies to ensure that grant funds are effectively spent.
- **Uncoordinated grant program creation:** Numerous federal grant programs have been created over time without coordinated purposes or scope. This can result in grants management challenges such as unnecessary duplication across grant programs and unnecessary overlap in funding.
- **Need for better collaboration:** A lack of collaboration among grant program participants can impede effective grant implementation in areas such as knowledge sharing and defining clear leadership roles.
- **Internal control weaknesses:** When internal controls in grants management and oversight are weak, federal grant-making agencies face challenges in achieving program goals and assuring the proper and effective use of federal funds. Effective controls can help to avoid improper grant payments.
- **Lack of agency or recipient capacity:** Capacity reflects the organizational, financial, and human capital resources available for the implementation of grant programs. A lack of capacity can adversely impact an agency's or recipient's ability to manage and implement grant programs.

ABBREVIATIONS

ACIR	U.S. Advisory Commission on Intergovernmental Relations
CFDA	Catalog of Federal Domestic Assistance
CFFR	Consolidated Federal Funds Report
CMS	Centers for Medicare & Medicaid Services
COFAR	Council on Financial Assistance Reform
CRS	Congressional Research Service
DHS	Department of Homeland Security
DOE	Department of Energy

Education	Department of Education
EECBG	Energy Efficiency and Conservation Block Grant
FAADS	Federal Assistance Awards Data System
FFATA	Federal Funding Accountability and Transparency Act
FEMA	Federal Emergency Management Agency
GDP	gross domestic product
GSA	General Services Administration
HHS	Department of Health and Human Services
HUD	Department of Housing and Urban Development
IG	Inspector General
JAG	Justice Assistance Grant
Justice	Department of Justice
NARA	National Archives and Records Administration
OMB	Office of Management and Budget
Recovery Act	American Recovery and Reinvestment Act of 2009
SHSP	State Homeland Security Program
UASI	Urban Areas Security Initiative

Congressional Requesters

Federal grants fund a wide array of activities. They help build and maintain our nation's infrastructure by funding highways, bridges, and mass transit systems. Grants help educate young people by supporting the construction of school buildings, the hiring of teachers, and increasing student access to higher education. They also help care for the sick and economically disadvantaged by funding medical services, nutrition programs, and housing assistance. Federal grants are diverse, varying greatly in both size and the grantees who receive them. Some can be small, such as a research grant from the National Science Foundation for less than a couple of thousand dollars, or they can be very large, such as Medicaid grants to individual states, which are worth billions of dollars. Grant recipients may include states and their agencies, local governments, tribal governments, nonprofit organizations, research institutions, or individuals. Regardless of these differences, Congress created the many varieties of grants to help meet national objectives. However, as the federal government faces deepening, long-term fiscal challenges, its ability to continue to support the current scope and breadth of federal grants will be a challenge.

In response to your request regarding the operation of federal grants, funding levels, and the challenges grant programs have faced, in this report we provide information on (1) the amount of grant funding to state and local governments for fiscal year 2011, how such funding has changed over the last three decades, difficulties related to identifying the number of such grant programs; and (2) selected grant challenges involving federal grants to state and local governments that have been identified in our previous work and that of federal inspectors general (IG) over the last several years.

In scoping the research objectives for this work we limited our review to federal grants involving state and local governments because reliable historical data exist for this group of grants and according to the Office of Management and Budget (OMB) they represent roughly 80 percent of all federal grant funding. We could not identify a similarly reliable data source for the wider universe of all federal grants.

To determine key information regarding grant funding for fiscal year 2011, the growth in grant funding over the last three decades, and shifts in the focus of grant funding during that time, we used data from OMB.[1] We obtained the data for fiscal years 1980 through 2011 and converted them to 2011 constant dollars for a more accurate comparison of grant spending from year to year.

We determined the data were sufficiently reliable for the purposes of this report. In addition to OMB, we identified other sources of data on federal grant funding, and then analyzed and described how the data in each source differs. In an effort to identify the number of grant programs, we looked at the Catalog of Federal Domestic Assistance (CFDA), a data base containing information on federal assistance programs. We also reviewed our prior work, and the work of others, on federal grants in the CFDA, reviewed studies by the Congressional Research Service, and discussed the issue with OMB and the General Services Administration (GSA).

To identify key issues and challenges related to the structure and operation of grants management, we reviewed our previous reports and audits as well as those from federal IGs and others. We also searched various federal, public policy, and research organizations' websites to identify relevant reports and other literature regarding federal grant programs and how they are structured and managed.

Finally, we discussed various issues related to federal grants and data on grant funding and programs with OMB and GSA, as these agencies have government-wide responsibilities related to grants, grants management, and grants data. Appendix I contains further information on our scope and methodology.

We conducted this performance audit from March 2012 to September 2012 in accordance with generally accepted government auditing standards. Those standards require that we plan and perform the audit to obtain sufficient, appropriate evidence to provide a reasonable basis for our findings and conclusions based on our audit objectives.

We believe that the evidence obtained provides a reasonable basis for our findings and conclusions based on our audit objectives.

BACKGROUND

Grants constitute one form of federal assistance consisting of payments in cash or in kind to a state or local government or a nongovernmental recipient for a specified purpose.[2] Taken as a whole, federal grant programs are extremely diverse. They can vary greatly in numerous ways including size, the nature of their recipients, and the type of programs they fund. Grant programs can also vary in two important dimensions— the amount of discretion they give to the recipient in how the funds will be used, and the way they are allocated or awarded.

Typically, grants are grouped into three types based on the amount of discretion given to the recipient for the use of funds: categorical grants, block grants, and general purpose grants.

- *Categorical grants* are the most restricted, permitting funds to be used only for specific activities related to their purpose, such as funding for the narrowly defined purpose of nutrition for the elderly.
- *Block grants* are less restrictive, funding broader categories of activities, such as community development or public health, and generally give greater discretion to recipients in identifying problems and designing programs to address those problems.
- *General purpose grants*, such as revenue sharing, offer the greatest amount of discretion to the recipient, as they require only that the funds be spent for government purposes.

However, grant categories with regard to categorical grants and block grants are not rigid and sometimes overlap occurs.[3] Each of these grants strikes a different balance between the interests of the federal grant-making agency that funds be used efficiently and effectively to meet national objectives, and the interests of the recipient to use the funds to meet local priorities and to minimize the administrative burdens associated with accepting the grant.

Grant programs also vary in the methods they use to allocate or award funds, that is, by formula or through discretionary project grants.

- *Formula grants* allocate funds based on distribution formulas prescribed by legislation or administrative regulation.
- *Project grants* are generally awarded on a competitive basis to eligible applicants for specific projects. OMB has emphasized the use of competitive grants as a means of increasing innovation in grant proposals.

While these labels help classify grants based on prominent characteristics, they should not be understood to be mutually exclusive definitions, as more than one can apply to a given grant program. For example, the federal government distributes Community Development Block Grant funds to states using a formula, but states redistribute the funds to localities, sometimes as project grants.

While there is substantial variation among grant types, competitive grants generally follow a life cycle that includes announcement, application, award, post-award, and closeout, as seen in figure 1. Once a grant program is established through legislation, which may specify particular objectives, eligibility, and other requirements, a grant-making agency may impose additional requirements on it. For competitive grant programs, the public is notified of the grant opportunity through an announcement, and potential recipients must submit applications for agency review. In the award stage, the agency identifies successful applicants or legislatively defined grant recipients and awards funding.

The implementation stage includes payment processing, agency monitoring, and recipient reporting, which may include financial and performance information.

The closeout phase includes preparation of final reports, financial reconciliation, and any required accounting for property. Audits may occur multiple times during the life cycle of the grant and after closeout.

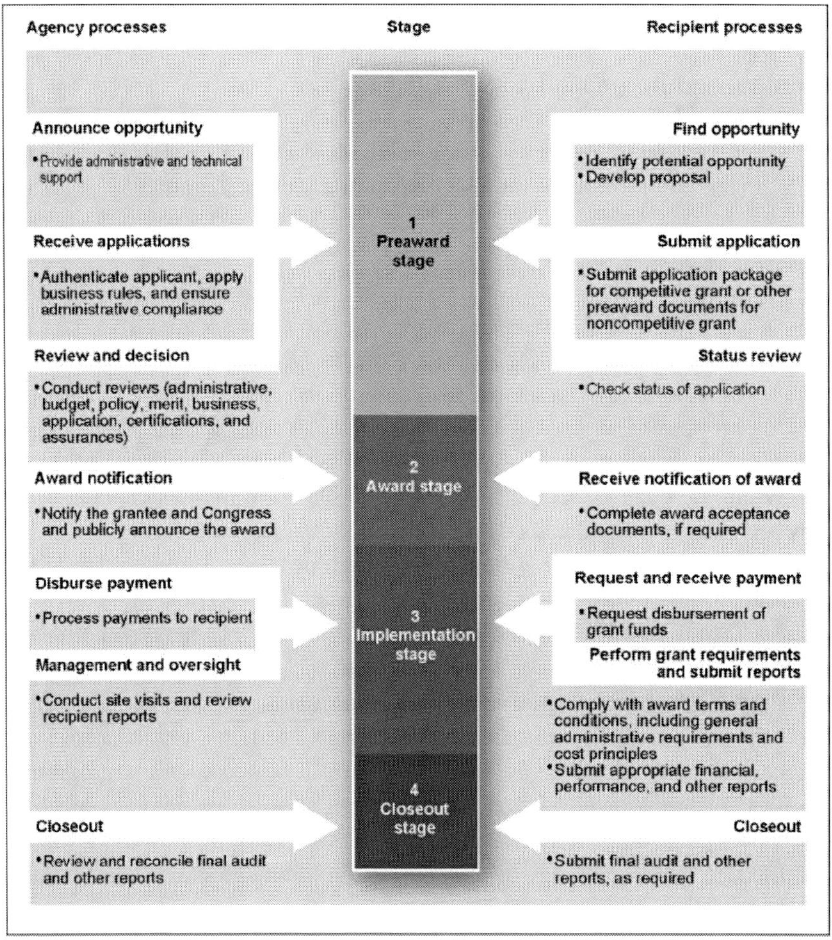

Source: GAO.

Figure 1. Grant Life Cycle of Federal Grant-making Agency and Grant Recipient.

Federal Grant Programs Are Established by Law and Subject to Many Different Legal Requirements

Federal agencies do not have inherent authority to enter into grant agreements without affirmative legislative authorization. In authorizing grant programs, federal laws identify the types of activities that can be funded and the purposes to be accomplished through the funding. Legislation establishing a grant program frequently will define the program objectives and leave the administering agency to fill in the details by regulation.

Grant programs are typically subject to a wide range of accountability requirements under their authorizing legislation or appropriation and implementing regulations so that funding is spent for its intended purpose. For example, the Department of Housing and Urban Development (HUD) administers grants to aid states and localities in providing affordable housing for low-income families. Congress mandated that HUD administer these grant programs in a manner that furthers fair housing. HUD regulations direct grant recipients to prepare planning documents and maintain certain records proving the legislation's fair housing requirements as a condition to receiving funds. Congress may also impose requirements on specific funding for grant programs. The American Recovery and Reinvestment Act of 2009 (Recovery Act) required increased reporting and oversight on both grant-making agencies and recipients for many different grant programs receiving additional funding under the Recovery Act.

Table 1. Government-wide and Program-Specific Grant Requirements

	Grant-making Agency	**Grant Recipient**
Specific to individual grant programs	Grant program's authorizing statute Appropriation act providing funding for grant program	Grant program regulations issued by grant-making agency Grant agreement (terms and conditions)
Applicable to all grant programs	Government-wide funding requirements Executive orders and OMB circulars on grants management	Government-wide grant regulations: (1) Administrative requirements ("common rule") (2) Cost principles (3) Drug-free workplace (4) Suspension and debarment (5) Anti-lobbying requirements (6) Audit and reporting requirements

Source: GAO.

In addition, grant programs are also subject to cross-cutting requirements applicable to most assistance programs (see table 1 for more information). For example, recipients of grant funds are prohibited from using those funds to lobby members and employees of Congress and executive agency employees. OMB is responsible for developing government-wide policies to ensure that grants are managed properly and that grant funds are spent in accordance with applicable laws and regulations. For many decades, OMB has published guidance in various circulars to aid grant-making agencies with such subjects as audit and record keeping and the allowability of costs. For a detailed discussion of grants management legislation and OMB's role in developing grants policy, see appendix III.

GRANTS TO STATE AND LOCAL GOVERNMENTS HAVE CONSISTENTLY BEEN A SIGNIFICANT COMPONENT OF FEDERAL SPENDING BUT THE FOCUS OF GRANT SPENDING HAS CHANGED OVER THE LAST THREE DECADES

Grants are an important tool used by the federal government to provide program funding to state and local governments. OMB has previously estimated that grants to state and local governments represent roughly 80 percent of all federal grant funding, with the remaining approximately 20 percent going to recipients such as nonprofit organizations, research institutions, or individuals. Federal outlays for grants to state and local governments totaled more than $606 billion in fiscal year 2011, equivalent to 4.1 percent of the gross domestic product (GDP) in that year. For comparison, federal outlays for national defense were 4.7 percent of GDP during the same period. With outlays of $275 billion in fiscal year 2011, Medicaid is by far the federal government's largest single grant program and by itself accounted for 45 percent of federal grant outlays to state and local governments in that year. The Department of Health and Human Services (HHS), which administers the Medicaid program, is the largest grant-making agency, with grant outlays of almost $348 billion in fiscal year 2011, or about 57 percent of the total federal grant outlays to state and local governments. However, even when Medicaid is excluded, HHS remains the largest federal grant-making agency. While many federal agencies award grants, the large majority of grant outlays to state and local governments are made by just a few agencies, with the top five accounting for more than 90 percent of those grant outlays in fiscal year 2011. Following HHS, the next four agencies with the largest amount of grant outlays to state and local governments in fiscal year 2011 were the Departments of Education (Education), Transportation, HUD, and Agriculture.

Figure 2 shows the amount of, and percentage of, grant outlays to state and local governments for the top 5 grant-making agencies.

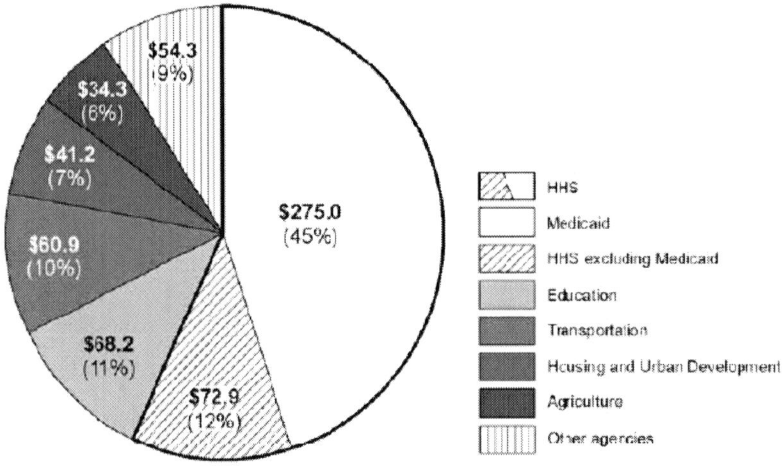

Source: GAO analysis of OMB data.

Figure 2. Amount and Percentage of Federal Outlays for Grants to State and Local Governments by Top Five Agencies, Fiscal Year 2011 (Dollars in Billions).

Federal outlays for grants to state and local governments increased from $91 billion in fiscal year 1980 (about $221 billion in 2011 constant dollars) to more than $606 billion in fiscal year 2011.[4] Figure 3 shows the total federal outlays for grants to state and local governments over the period from fiscal years 1980 to 2011, in constant dollars, and the increasing amount of this total that went to Medicaid over time.

While the past three decades have witnessed a dramatic growth in federal grants to state and local governments in absolute dollar terms, the same is not true when one considers these grant outlays as a proportion of total federal spending. As shown in figure 4, grant outlays to state and local governments as a percentage of total federal outlays in fiscal year 2011 were at a roughly comparable level to what they were more than 30 years earlier (16.8 percent versus 15.5 percent).[5] However, during this period the proportion of federal grant outlays to state and local governments dedicated to Medicaid more than tripled, rising from 2.4 percent of all federal outlays in 1980 to 7.6 percent in 2011. The increase in outlays for Medicaid and other health-related grant programs was offset by an approximately equivalent decrease in the share of outlays for other grants to state and local governments.

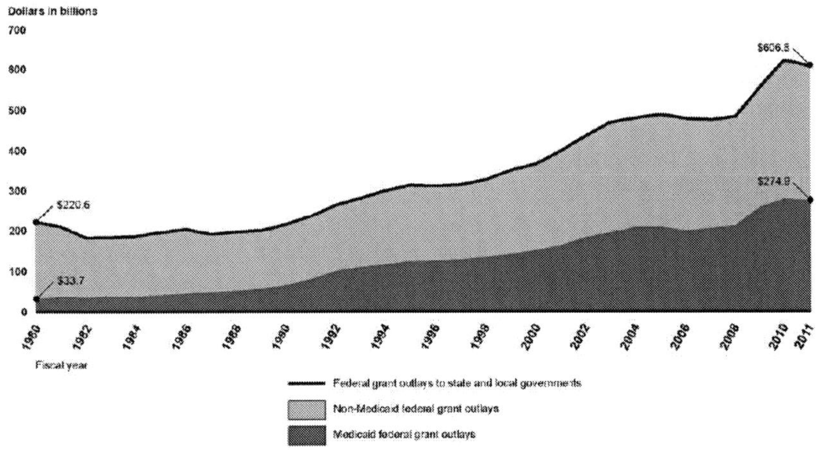

Source: GAO analysis of OMB data.

Figure 3. Federal Outlays for Grants to State and Local Governments and Medicaid, in 2011 Constant Dollars, Fiscal Years 1980 to 2011.

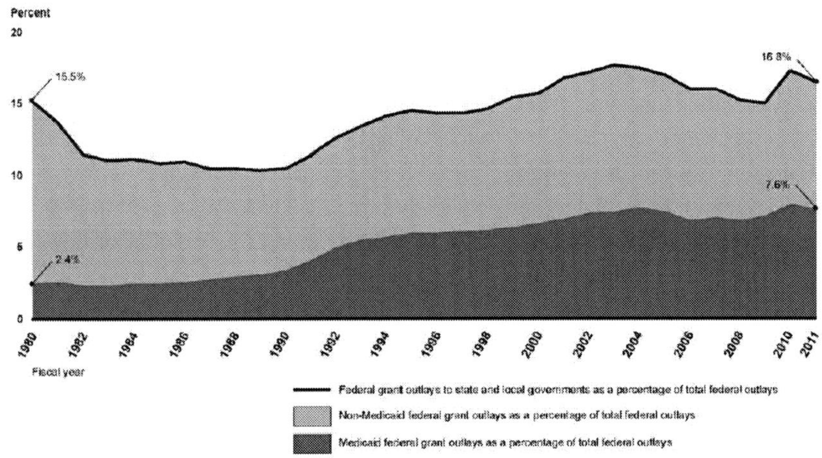

Source: GAO analysis of OMB data.

Figure 4. Federal Outlays for Grants to State and Local Governments and Medicaid as a Percentage of Total Federal Outlays, Fiscal Years 1980 to 2011.

The dip in federal grant outlays to state and local governments as a percentage of total outlays during the 1980s, seen in figure 4, was likely due to a variety of factors, including efforts undertaken at the time to merge categorical grant programs in several functional areas into block grants and also reduce funding levels. For example, as part of the Omnibus Budget Reconciliation Act of 1981, nine block grants were created from about 50 of the 534 categorical programs in effect at that time. Overall, funding for the categorical grants bundled into these block grants was reduced 12 percent, about $1 billion, from their combined funding level the previous year. State officials believed that funding reductions would not result in the loss of services for recipients because the reductions would be offset by administrative efficiencies, although in our subsequent work we found that the administrative cost savings were difficult to quantify.[6] Figure 4 also shows the upturn in federal grant outlays in 2009 and 2010 that were the result of the Recovery Act.

Grant outlays can also be analyzed historically using OMB's grant programs' functional categories. In fiscal year 2011, the five largest grant program categories by government function were health; income security; education, training, employment, and social services; transportation; and community and regional development. Figure 5 shows federal grant outlays to state and local governments broken out by these five governmental functions, from fiscal year 1980 to fiscal year 2011.

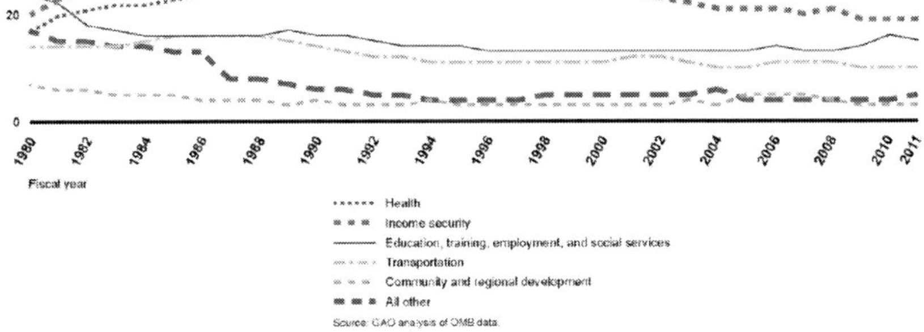

Source: GAO analysis of OMB data.

Figure 5. Federal Outlays for Grants to State and Local Governments by Top Five Functions as a Percentage of Total Federal Grants Outlays, Fiscal Years 1980 to 2011.

Health function grant outlays were 17 percent of total grant outlays to state and local governments in fiscal year 1980—lower than either income security or education.[7] By fiscal year 2011, outlays for health-related grant functions increased to almost 50 percent of these total grant outlays. While outlays for health-related grants experienced a relatively steady increase in the last three decades—more than doubling in 30 years—outlays for other grant functions generally decreased relative to the total of all federal grants to state and local governments during the same period.

OMB and others have noted that the relative growth and contraction of grant outlays for different purposes reflects a broader shift in the focus of federal outlays for grant programs. According to OMB data, since the 1980s, funding has shifted from providing grants to state and local governments for physical capital and societal activities (e.g., highways, mass transit, sewage treatment plants, public education, government administration and community development), toward grants for payments for the benefit of individuals or families. These grants benefitting individuals are primarily entitlement programs such as Medicaid, Temporary Assistance for Needy Families, child nutrition programs, and housing assistance. In fiscal year 1980, the percentage of grant outlays for the benefit of individuals and families was just under 36 percent. By fiscal year 2011, federal outlays for grants benefitting individuals and families, a major component of which is Medicaid, had grown to almost two-thirds (64 percent) of all grant outlays to state and local governments.

There are various sources for data on the amount the federal government spends on grants, including OMB budget data, USAspending.gov, and Census Bureau surveys of state and local governments. See appendix II for more detail about these data sources and their differences. The various differences in each data source can create challenges for those examining federal grants management issues and for congressional oversight of grants administration.

While the Number of Federal Grant Programs Has Generally Increased over the Last Three Decades, a Definitive Figure Is Not Available

Our prior work and the work of others have shown that the number of federal grant programs to state and local governments has generally increased over the last three decades. However, determining a definitive number of federal grant programs presents certain difficulties. Efforts to accurately track the number of federal grant programs over time have been complicated by the fact that different entities have counted grant programs differently for decades. Both OMB and the former U.S. Advisory Commission on Intergovernmental Relations (ACIR) periodically published counts of the total number of federally funded grant programs during the 1980s and 1990s, but because they used different methodologies to determine which grant programs to include, they came up with different results. For example, in 1995 OMB identified 608 federally funded grant programs compared to ACIR's count of 633.[8] OMB no longer issues formal counts of federally funded grant programs and there is no current consensus on the methodology used to count federal grant programs.

Although the CFDA is the single authoritative, government-wide compendium and source document for descriptions of federal programs that provide assistance or benefits to the public, as the experiences of OMB and ACIR suggest, a simple tally of the CFDA database will not provide an accurate count of the number of federally funded grant programs. 9 This is due to a number of reasons. First, according to GSA officials, there is not a one-to-one relationship between individual grant program opportunities and overarching CFDA programs. Multiple grant programs can trace their legal authority back to a single CFDA program description and CFDA number. CFDA programs contain broader objectives than individual grant opportunities. Second, not all of the programs listed in the CFDA have current appropriations. CFDA is a catalog containing active funded and inactive non-funded programs which have been archived at an agency's request. Third, officials from GSA told us that each agency determines how to organize and describe their programs for publication in the CFDA, as long as the agency adheres to the underlying requirement to describe the program's legal authority, administering office, funding, purpose, benefits, and beneficiaries. These are among the many factors that complicate efforts to accurately count the number of federal grant programs using the information included in the CFDA database.

Grants Challenges Reflect the Diversity and Complexity of Grants Management for State and Local Governments

Over time, growth of both the numbers of grant programs for state and local governments and their level of funding has created greater diversity and complexity in federal grants management. Substantial variation in the way federal agencies administer these programs has further increased their complexity. As a result, the management of grants to state and local governments presents both grant-making agencies and grant recipients with a variety of challenges. We and others have previously reported on many of these issues which can be grouped into the following broad themes: (1) challenges related to effectively measuring grant performance; (2) uncoordinated program creation; (3) need for better collaboration; (4) internal control weaknesses in grants management and oversight; and (5) lack of agency or recipient capacity.

Lack of Appropriate Performance Measures and Accurate Data Limit Agencies' Ability to Effectively Measure Grant Program Performance

In our past work, we have reported that effective performance accountability provisions are of fundamental importance in assuring the proper and effective use of federal funds and determining if grant program goals are met. Two issues that we have previously identified as important for effectively reporting on grant performance are having appropriate, high-quality performance measures and accurate performance data.[10]

Lack of Appropriate Performance Measures

While the principles of good governance indicate that agencies should establish performance measures to demonstrate how they intend to achieve their program goals and measure the extent to which they have done so, selecting the measures by which a grant program's performance is assessed can be challenging.[11] We have previously reported on the general attributes of appropriate grant performance measures, noting that measures should be linked to agency goals and missions; be clearly stated; include measurable targets; and be objective, reliable, and balanced. However, we have found that while agencies may implement measures with some of these attributes, other key attributes may not be incorporated. For example, the Department of Justice (Justice) developed and implemented 86 new performance measures for the Edward Byrne Memorial Justice Assistance Grant (JAG) funds to state and local governments for criminal justice activities in 2009. While Justice continued to make efforts to improve these measures in 2009, we reported that 19 of the JAG performance measures we reviewed generally lacked, in varying degrees, several key attributes of successful performance measurement systems, including clarity, linkages with strategic or programmatic goals, objectivity, reliability, and the measurability of targets.[12] Specifically, we found that 14 of the 19 measures were not clearly defined; 14 of the 19 measures were not linked to Justice's strategic or programmatic goals; 13 of the 19 measures were not reliable; and 17 of the 19 measures did not have measurable targets. Our report noted that by more fully incorporating such attributes of effective performance measures into its performance measurement and reporting system, Justice could facilitate accountability, be better positioned to monitor and assess results, and subsequently improve its grants management. We recommended that Justice should, in revising its performance measures, consider incorporating key attributes of successful performance measurement systems, such as clarity, reliability, linkage, objectivity, and measurable targets. Justice concurred with the recommendations in our report and they have actions underway that address the recommendations.

In another example of an agency's publishing measures that do not necessarily contribute to its ability to assess grant program effectiveness, Department of Homeland Security (DHS) implemented some performance measures for the State Homeland Security Program (SHSP) and Urban Areas Security Initiative (UASI) in the fiscal year 2011 grant guidance.

However, the type of measures DHS published in the SHSP and UASI guidance did not contribute to DHS's ability to assess the effectiveness of these grant programs, but instead provided DHS with information to help it measure completion of tasks or activities. We recommended, among other things, that DHS revise its plan to ensure the timely implementation of performance measures to assess the effectiveness of these grants.

According to DHS, it has efforts under way to develop additional measures to help it assess grant program effectiveness; however, until these measures are implemented, it will be difficult for DHS to determine the effectiveness of these grant-funded projects, which totaled $20.3 billion from fiscal years 2002 through 2011.[13] As we have previously reported, performance measures that evaluate program results can help Congress make more informed policy decisions regarding program achievements and performance. Agencies could facilitate accountability, be better positioned to monitor and assess results, and subsequently improve their grants management by including key attributes of successful performance measurement systems in their performance measure revisions.

Data Collection and Validation Challenges

Grant programs often rely on recipients' administrative systems to provide performance information. Our prior work has shown that agencies relying on third parties for performance data can have difficulty collecting the data as well as ascertaining its accuracy and quality. In past work, we have also found that the availability and credibility of performance data has been a long-standing weakness. An example of this can be seen in our November 2011 report on federal "green building" initiatives that foster—in part through the use of grant funds—construction and maintenance practices designed to make efficient use of resources, reduce environmental problems, and provide long-term financial and health benefits in the nonfederal sector. Eleven agencies implemented 94 federal initiatives, 47 of which were funded by grants. Agency officials reported that they may not have had information on the results of green building initiatives for the nonfederal sector, in part because they faced several challenges in gathering appropriate and reliable performance data, such as utility usage data for multifamily properties. These difficulties included obtaining the resources necessary to develop systems for accurate data collection, a lack of industry standards for performance data collection, third party utility companies' diverse policies governing data sharing, as well as the utility companies' wide-ranging capacities to collect data. In particular, HUD officials told us the quality of utility data can vary by utility company, especially for water consumption data—which can be incomplete and inaccurate and is often not available in electronic form.[14]

In other instances, actual performance data may not be available until after the completion of the grant project. For example, Department of Energy (DOE) officials said that for the Energy Efficiency and Conservation Block Grant program (EECBG) actual energy savings data are generally available only after a project is completed; therefore, to comply with the program's reporting requirements, most recipients reported estimates calculated using the Environmental Protection Agency's Portfolio Manager tool. While DOE officials said they had anecdotal examples of program successes, DOE had experienced challenges in assessing the reasonableness of the energy-savings estimates provided by recipients because DOE did not require recipients to use the most up-to-date estimating tool when calculating and reporting energy-savings estimates. Consequently, DOE could not identify instances where recipients' estimates may need to be more carefully reviewed.[15] We recommended, among other things, that DOE should solicit information on recipients' methods for estimating energy savings and verify that recipients use the most recent version of the estimating tool. To address our recommendation, DOE issued guidance effective June 23, 2011, that eliminates the requirement for grant recipients to calculate and report estimated energy savings. DOE officials said the calculation of estimated impact metrics will now be performed centrally by DOE by applying known national standards to existing grantee-reported performance metrics. Based on DOE's action, we concluded that DOE has addressed the intent of this recommendation. Even in federal grants with designs that favor performance accountability, challenges related to collecting and reporting performance data can affect the extent to which performance accountability can be achieved.

Numerous Federal Grant Programs, Created over Time without Coordinated Purposes and Scopes, Can Result in Grants Management Challenges

In our *2012 Annual Report: Opportunities to Reduce Duplication, Overlap and Fragmentation, Achieve Savings, and Enhance Revenue*, we reported on examples of how multiple federal grant programs, created without coordinated purposes and scopes, can result in structural grants management challenges.[16] One example involved four DHS grant programs—the State Homeland Security Program, the Urban Areas Security Initiative, the Port Security Grant Program, and the Transit Security Grant Program. DHS's Federal Emergency Management Agency (FEMA) allocated about $20.3 billion to recipients through the four programs from fiscal years 2002 through 2011. These four grant programs have similar goals and fund similar activities in overlapping jurisdictions. For instance, many jurisdictions within designated Urban Areas Security Initiative regions also apply for and receive State Homeland Security Program funding. Similarly, port stakeholders in urban areas could receive funding for equipment such as patrol boats through both the Port Security Grant Program and the Urban Areas Security Initiative, and a transit agency could purchase surveillance equipment with Transit Security Grant Program or Urban Areas Security Initiative funding. We, as well as DHS's IG, concluded that FEMA should use more specific project-level data in making grant award decisions in order to identify and mitigate potential duplication. Our work, and the work of the DHS IG, concluded that coordinating the review of grant projects internally would give FEMA more complete information about applications across the four grant programs that could help FEMA identify and mitigate the risk of unnecessary duplication across grant applications.[17] We recommended in February 2012, among other things, that FEMA take steps to ensure that it collects project information with the level of detail needed to better position the agency to identify any potential unnecessary duplication within and across the four grant programs. DHS concurred with our recommendation in this area.

In another example of this challenge, we found instances where Justice could improve how it targets nearly $3.9 billion to reduce the risk of potentially unnecessary duplication across more than 11,000 grant awards it makes annually. Justice's grant-making agencies had awarded funds from different grant programs to the same applicants whose applications described similar—and in some cases, the same—purposes for using the grant funds. While we acknowledged that there may be times when Justice's decision to fund recipients in this manner is warranted, our work found that Justice made grant award decisions without visibility over whether the funds supported similar or the same purposes, thus potentially resulting in unintended, and unnecessary, duplication. We found that Justice had not assessed its grant programs to determine the extent to which they may overlap with one another and determine if consolidation of grant programs may be appropriate. Further, Justice's grant-making agencies had not established consistent policies and procedures for sharing grant application information that could help them identify and mitigate unnecessary duplication in how recipients intend to use their grant awards.[18] We recommended that Justice should conduct an assessment to better understand the extent to which the department's grant programs overlap with one another and determine if grant programs may be consolidated to mitigate the risk of unnecessary duplication. To the extent that Justice identifies any statutory obstacles to consolidating its grant programs, it should work with Congress to address them, as needed. Justice concurred with our recommendations in this area. Addressing structural challenges such as these may achieve cost savings, enhance revenue, and could result in greater efficiencies in grant programs.

Because of Its Complexity, Grants Management Benefits from Effective Collaboration among Intergovernmental and Nongovernmental Participants

The process of distributing federal assistance through grants is complicated and involves many different parties—both public and private—with different organizational structures, sizes, and missions. In previous work, we have identified lack of collaboration among and between federal agencies, state and local governments, and nongovernmental grant participants as a challenge to effective grant implementation.[19] Because grants management can be complex, collaboration among the grant participants, particularly with regard to information sharing, is important. With this in mind, we have identified key practices to enhance and sustain collaboration among federal agencies.[20] We have also recommended these same key practices to strengthen partnerships between government and nongovernmental entities, such as nonprofit organizations.[21] In that same report, we describe an example related to hurricane recovery that involves difficulties in collaboration between federal agencies and state and local case management providers. Disaster case management is a process that assists people in identifying their service needs, locating and arranging services, and coordinating the services of multiple providers to help people recover from a disaster. State and local agencies providing federally funded disaster case management services faced challenges in, among other things, obtaining timely and accurate information from the federal agencies overseeing the disaster case management programs. While FEMA had a lead role in coordinating other types of disaster assistance after Hurricanes Katrina and Rita, its role for coordinating disaster case management was not explicit. Initial coordination activities among federal agencies and case management providers were minimal following the hurricanes. As a result, we found that some victims may not have received case management services while others may have received services from multiple providers.[22] We recommended, among other things, that FEMA establish a time line for developing a disaster case management program that includes practices to enhance coordination among stakeholders involved in this program. FEMA agreed with our recommendations in this area and reported that it would take steps to coordinate with stakeholders. Among other actions, FEMA has since held a disaster case management summit, and participants made recommendations for improving coordination among federal and nonfederal stakeholders that will be included in the disaster case management program guidance.

In another example of collaboration challenges, 80 federal grant programs are authorized to provide funding for transportation for disadvantaged populations and involve several federal agencies, including the Departments of Agriculture, Education, HHS, HUD, Interior, Labor, Transportation, and Veterans Affairs. [23] These grantors may provide funds to state and local agencies that can be used for transportation expenses to help individuals access federal programs, including education, employment, medical care, or other human services.[24] To improve the efficiency and effectiveness of human services transportation by coordinating related programs at the federal level and promoting the maximum feasible coordination at the state and local levels, the federal grant-making agencies collaborate through an Interagency Transportation Coordinating Council on Access and Mobility (Coordinating Council). In our past work we have reported that while some collaboration efforts have shown promising results, obstacles continued to impede other attempts at collaboration between grant participants.[25] In 2011, we reported that while some federal agencies were developing guidance and technical assistance for transportation coordination, other federal departments still had more work to do in identifying and assessing their transportation programs, working with other federal departments to identify opportunities for additional collaboration, and developing and disseminating policies and recipient guidance for coordinating transportation services.[26] In June 2012, we reported that several state and local officials told us that there was not sufficient federal leadership and guidance on how to coordinate transportation services for the disadvantaged and that varying federal program requirements may hinder coordination of transportation services, acting as barriers to collaboration. In that report, we recommended that in order to promote and enhance federal, state, and local coordination activities, the Secretary of Transportation as the chair of the Coordinating Council, as well as the member agencies of the Coordinating Council, should complete and publish a strategic plan and report on their progress in implementing their recommendations. Education and Veterans Affairs generally agreed with our report, while HHS, HUD, and the Department of Transportation neither agreed nor disagreed.

Internal Control Weaknesses in Grants Management and Oversight Processes Affect Federal Agencies' Ability to Ensure Grant Funds Are Spent Effectively

When awarding and managing federal grants, effective oversight and internal control is important to provide reasonable assurance to federal managers and taxpayers that grants are awarded properly, recipients are eligible, and federal grant funds are used as intended and in accordance with applicable laws and regulations. Internal control comprises the plans, methods, and procedures agencies use to be reasonably assured that their missions, goals, and objectives can be met. In numerous reviews over the years, we and agency IGs have identified weaknesses in agencies' internal controls for managing and overseeing grants. When such controls are weak, federal grant-making agencies face challenges in achieving grant program goals and assuring the proper and effective use of federal funds which can help avoid improper payments.

Control Weaknesses in Monitoring and Overseeing Grant Programs

Agencies are responsible for overseeing and monitoring implementation of their grant programs to help ensure that recipients are meeting program and accountability requirements. Oversight procedures for monitoring the recipients' use of awarded funds, including site visits and review of recipient reports, can help agencies determine whether recipients are operating efficiently and effectively and whether program funds are being spent appropriately. Risk-based monitoring programs can help identify those areas in need of oversight resources. When agencies do not consider certain risk factors when selecting recipients for site visits, they may not know where to focus their monitoring resources. For example, in February 2011, the IG at the National Archives and Records Administration (NARA) reported that NARA, among other things, had not developed a risk-based process for monitoring and determining which grants to review.[27] The IG found that NARA did not consider relevant factors, such as a program's age or size, or the experience of the recipient. The IG concluded that without a more structured process for determining and assessing risk, NARA could not provide adequate assurance that risks associated with its grant programs are properly addressed and mitigated. According to the IG, NARA subsequently took corrective actions, including developing selection criteria for grantee site visits and desk audits and determining their frequency.

Federal agencies award grant funds to recipients, often states and local governments, and then those grant recipients may award, or pass through, subgrants to subrecipients. [28] It is important that grant recipients identify, prioritize, and manage potential at-risk subrecipients to ensure that grant goals are reached and funds are used properly. In April 2011, we reported on DOE's use of Recovery Act funds for the EECBG program. [29] We found that EECBG recipients used various methods to monitor sub-recipients, with some recipients providing more rigorous monitoring than others. DOE officials acknowledged that many recipients are resource constrained, limiting their ability to monitor subrecipients and ensure compliance with applicable federal requirements. DOE gathered specific information on recipient monitoring practices during on-site visits.

However, because not all recipients were to receive site visits, DOE did not have specific information on monitoring for many recipients, and therefore, did not know whether those monitoring activities were sufficiently rigorous to ensure compliance with federal requirements. We recommended that DOE explore a means to capture information on the monitoring processes of all recipients to make certain that recipients have effective monitoring practices. DOE has taken some actions to increase their monitoring efforts; however, the actions may not result in capturing information on the monitoring practices of all recipients.

Medicaid, the largest federal grant program, has also been the subject of numerous reviews. The challenges faced by HHS's Centers for Medicare & Medicaid Services (CMS) in overseeing fiscal management of the Medicaid program have been well-documented in our past work.[30] Because of concerns about the program's fiscal management, size, growth, and diversity, Medicaid has been on our list of high-risk programs. Areas of concern in the Medicaid program include improper payments and inconsistent reviews of managed care rate setting by CMS.

Government-wide Issues

Our work has identified weaknesses in grant oversight and accountability issues that span the government, including challenges in oversight of undisbursed grant award balances and significant levels of improper payments in grant programs.

We have found issues and raised concerns about timely grant closeouts, including undisbursed funds remaining in grant accounts, across the federal government. For grant programs with a defined end date, closeout procedures help ensure that grant recipients have met all financial requirements, provided final reports, and returned any unused funds. We have reported that some agencies lack adequate systems or policies to properly monitor grant closeouts or did not deobligate funds from grants eligible for closeout in a timely manner.[31] When agencies do not conduct closeout procedures in a timely manner, unused funds can be prevented from being used to help address the purpose of the grant. Further, failure to close out a grant and deobligate any unspent balances can allow recipients to continue to draw down federal funds even after the grant's period of availability to the recipient has ended, making these funds more susceptible to waste, fraud, or mismanagement. In April 2012, we reported that, as of September 30, 2011, more than $794 million remained in expired grant accounts in the Payment Management System, the largest civilian federal payment system which made 68 percent of all federal grant disbursements in fiscal year 2010.[32] These accounts were more than 3 months past the grant end date and had no activity for 9 months or more, with some balances remaining in grant accounts several years past their expiration date. Subsequently, OMB issued guidance instructing federal agencies to take appropriate action to close out grants in a timely manner.

Federal agencies reported an estimated $115.3 billion in improper payments in fiscal year 2011. Many of the programs reporting improper payments were federal grant programs, including Medicaid and the National School Lunch program. Strong preventive controls are important as they serve as the front-line defense against improper payments, and effective monitoring and reporting are important to help detect emerging improper payment issues. In March 2012, we reported that many agencies and programs are in the process of implementing preventive controls that involve activities such as training, which can be a key element in any effort to prevent improper payments from occurring.[33] For example, CMS's Medicaid Integrity Group trains state-level staff and sponsors education programs for beneficiaries and providers. Along with strong preventive controls, effective detection techniques, such as data mining and recovery auditing to quickly identify and recover improper payments, are important for reducing improper payments.

In addition to weaknesses and issues found in our and IG reviews of agencies' grants-related controls and individual grant programs, we identified grants management as a significant deficiency in internal control in our fiscal year 2011 audit of the consolidated financial statements for the U.S. Government.[34] A deficiency in internal control exists when the design or operation of a control does not allow management or employees, in the normal course of performing their assigned functions, to prevent or detect and correct misstatements on a timely basis.[35]

We reported that these internal control deficiencies could adversely affect the federal government's ability to ensure that grant funds are being spent in accordance with applicable program laws and regulations. We based our finding on audits of agencies' fiscal year 2011 financial statements, where auditors at several federal agencies found grants management internal control deficiencies, primarily regarding inadequate monitoring and oversight of grant programs. For example, the auditor at HUD reported issues regarding timely action and follow-up with noncompliant recipients, as well as inadequate procedures to identify noncompliant recipients. We reported that these internal control deficiencies could adversely affect the federal government's ability to ensure that grant funds are being spent in accordance with applicable program laws and regulations.

A Lack of Organizational, Financial, or Human Capital Capacity Impacts the Ability of Grant-making Agencies and Recipients to Effectively Manage Grant Programs

The capacity of grant-making agencies and recipients is a key issue in grants management which can impact program success. Capacity involves both the maintenance of appropriate resources and the ability to effectively manage those resources. Building sufficient capacity is a challenge that may involve significant costs or tradeoffs. Three relevant types of capacity are organizational, human capital, and financial.

Organizational capacity captures the degree to which the grant-making agency or recipient is institutionally prepared for grants management and implementation. This may include having appropriate leadership, management structure, and size to efficiently and effectively implement the program and adapt as needed.

For example, we recently reported that capacity was a concern for states, school districts, and schools in the School Improvement Grant program.[36] States and districts both struggled to develop the necessary staff capacity to successfully support and oversee the program implementation because of resource constraints.

Officials from Education and several states told us that the grant required states to support local reform efforts to a much greater extent than they had in the past, and staff in some states had not yet developed the knowledge base to fulfill these responsibilities. Some states noted that such capacity limitations meant that time staff could devote to administering the program and monitoring district implementation was significantly limited.

Human capital capacity measures the extent to which an organization has sufficient staff, knowledge, and technical skills to effectively meet its program goals. Human capital needs shift over time as programs change and face new challenges.

Human capital needs also shift as new technology is implemented and the organization finds new ways to leverage expertise. Human capital challenges at the federal, state, and local level can underlie the operational difficulties faced during program implementation. For example, we have previously reported that during the initial phases of Gulf Coast rebuilding following the hurricanes in 2005, officials at both the federal and state level initially lacked the human capital capacity to administer the public assistance grant program.[37]

In addition, local applicants initially lacked the staff to fully participate as partners in the program. Shortages of staff with the right skills and abilities, as well as the lack of continuity among rotating FEMA staff, contributed to delays in developing public assistance projects in Louisiana and Mississippi.

Insufficient financial resources at the grant-making agency or recipient to administer or implement the grant can also limit the effectiveness of a grant in a number of ways. Financial capacity constraints may lead some recipients, such as nonprofits, to reduce the population served, the scope of services offered, and possibly forgo or delay physical infrastructure and technology improvements and staffing needs.

We have previously reported that because many nonprofits view cuts in clients served or services offered as unpalatable, they have reported that they often compromise vital "back-office" functions, which over time can affect their ability to meet their missions.[38] Further, nonprofits' strained resources limit their ability to build a financial safety net, which can create a precarious financial situation for them.

Absent a sufficient safety net, nonprofits that experience delays in receiving their federal funding may be inhibited in their ability to bridge funding gaps. When funding is delayed, some nonprofits have reported that they either borrow funds on a line of credit or use cash reserves to provide services and pay bills until their grant awards are received. Collectively, these issues place stress on the nonprofit sector, diminishing its ability to continue to effectively partner with the federal government to provide services to vulnerable populations.

Since this report does not contain any new audit work that evaluates the policies or operations of any federal agency in this report, we did not seek agency comments.

However, because of the role of OMB and GSA in producing or managing data on grant outlays and the number of grant programs, we shared drafts of relevant excerpts of this report with cognizant officials at these agencies and we made technical clarifications where appropriate.

Stanley J. Czerwinski Director,
Strategic Issues

Beryl H. Davis
Director,
Financial Management and Assurance

APPENDIX I: OBJECTIVES, SCOPE, AND METHODOLOGY

Our objectives were to describe (1) the amount of grant funding to state and local governments for fiscal year 2011, how grant funding to state and local governments has changed over the last three decades, and difficulties related to identifying the number of such grant programs; and (2) selected grant challenges involving federal grants to state and local governments that have been identified in our previous work and that of federal inspectors general (IG) over the last several years.

In scoping the research objectives for this work we decided to limit our review to federal grants involving state and local governments because reliable historical data exist for this group of grants and, according to the Office of Management and Budget (OMB), such grants represent roughly 80 percent of all federal grant funding. We could not identify a similarly-reliable data source for the wider universe of all federal grants. To do this work we took the actions described below and we discussed various issues related to federal grants and data on grants funding and programs with officials at the OMB and the General Services Administration (GSA), as these agencies have government-wide responsibilities related to grants, grants management, and grants data.

To determine key information regarding grant funding for fiscal year 2011, the growth in grant funding over the last three decades, and shifts in the focus of grant funding during that time, we used OMB data, specifically, OMB's Historical Table 12.3, *Total Outlays for Grants to State and Local Governments, by Function, Agency, and Program: 1940 – 2013* and Table 12.2, *Total Outlays for Grants to State and Local Governments, by Function and Fund Group: 1940 – 2017*.

We extracted the data for fiscal years 1980 through 2011 and converted each fiscal year's outlay amount to 2011 constant dollars which reflect adjustments for inflation. We sorted the data by agency and budget function (i.e., purpose of the spending) to identify the top five grant-making agencies and the top five functions for which grants were awarded. To determine grant outlays as a percentage of total outlays, we also used OMB's Historical Table 6.1, *Composition of Outlays: 1940-2017*. As these are budget data that has undergone rigorous review by OMB, they are generally considered sufficiently reliable for most of our purposes. Therefore, we determined the data were sufficiently reliable for the purposes of this report.

To describe issues related to identifying the number of grant programs, we reviewed our prior work and the work of others on federal grants and the

Catalog of Federal Domestic Assistance (CFDA), the single authoritative, government-wide compendium and source for descriptions of federal programs that provide assistance or benefits to the American public. We reviewed research regarding methodologies used to count grant programs published by the Congressional Research Service (CRS). We discussed issues related to CFDA numbers and their relationship to the number of grant programs with GSA, the agency responsible for maintaining CFDA. We also inquired into issues regarding counting the number of grant programs with OMB. The on-line version, www.CFDA.gov, allows one to search for assistance programs using a number of search options, including the federal agency providing the assistance, program name, and assistance type.[1]

In addition to the OMB data described above, we identified other sources of data for information on the amounts of federal grants funding, including USASpending.gov and Census Bureau data. We analyzed and compared the different sources and describe how the data elements in each source differ. We discussed issues relating to USASpending.gov, including the reliability of the data, with GSA, the agency responsible for maintaining it. See appendix II for details about the data sources we identified and how they differ.

To identify key issues and challenges related to the structure and operation of grants management, we reviewed previous relevant reports and audits by us, federal inspectors general (IG), and others. We searched GAO's online database for grants management-related reports from 1995 to the present, and reviewed selected relevant reports. To identify more recent issues and challenges for the examples in this report, we reviewed selected GAO reports from 2006 to 2012.

For IG reports, we searched websites for IGs of large and small grant-making agencies for reports related to grants management and financial statement audit reports where internal control weaknesses are identified. We determined whether the issues and challenges we identified still existed by reviewing our recommendation follow up work. For reports by others, we researched follow up work by the applicable IGs. We also searched various federal, public policy, and research organizations' websites, including those for the CRS and OMB, to identify relevant reports and other literature regarding federal grant programs and how they are structured and managed.

We shared drafts of the relevant sections of this report with cognizant officials at OMB and GSA. They generally agreed with the contents of this report and we incorporated their technical clarifications where appropriate.

Appendix II: Sources of Information on Grants

Various sources exist for data on the amount the federal government spends on grants, including Office of Management and Budget (OMB) budget data, USASpending.gov, and Census Bureau surveys of state and local governments. Each source was established and is used for slightly different purposes and contains different data elements. The various differences in each data source can create challenges for those examining federal grants management issues when trying to identify the scope of federal spending on grants. This appendix explains the purposes for and the differences in data contained in each source.

OMB Budget Data

OMB collects data from federal agencies each year to prepare the President's budget. OMB uses this data for a number of purposes related to the budget, including producing *Historical Tables* and *Analytical Perspectives*. One series of *Historical Tables* contains information on federal outlays for grants to state and local governments. According to OMB, the purpose of this series of *Historical Tables* is to identify federal government outlays that constitute income to state and local governments to help finance their services. *Analytical Perspectives*, according to OMB, is designed to highlight specific subject areas or provide other presentations of budget data that put the budget in context.

USASpending.gov

In response to the Federal Funding Accountability and Transparency Act (FFATA), OMB established USASpending.gov in December 2007 to enhance the transparency of government expenditures.[1] FFATA required that OMB establish a publicly available online database that would allow users to search for detailed information about entities that are awarded federal grants, loans, contracts, and other forms of financial assistance. The Congressional Research Service (CRS) reported that the premise of the law was that by making details of federal spending available to the public, government officials would be less likely to fund projects that might be perceived as wasteful. In addition, the new database required by the law would also help citizens better understand how the government distributes funds.[2] For grant awards, federal agencies report the amount of obligations they incur and information on the recipients of those awards, starting in fiscal year 2007, in accordance with OMB guidance for agency data submissions.[3] Over 490,000 grant-related transactions were reported by federal agencies for fiscal year 2011.

Census Bureau Surveys

The Census Bureau collects data from state and local governments, including data on grants provided by the federal government. This census of governments is one component of the nation's economic census required by law, 4 and provides, among other things, periodic and comprehensive statistics about governments and their financial activities.

Consolidated Federal Funds Report

Prior to fiscal year 2011, the annual Consolidated Federal Funds Report (CFFR) was prepared by the Census Bureau from data submitted by federal agencies to the Federal Assistance Awards Data System (FAADS) and other selected agency data. With the enactment of FFATA, which required agencies to report data elements in addition to those that were captured by FAADS, and due to funding issues, the Census Bureau stopped publishing the CFFR after the fiscal year 2010 report. The information is now available for the public to review on USASpending.gov. Table 2 summarizes data elements included and not included in these data sources and provides more information about them.

Table 2. Information about the Sources for Data on Federal Spending on Grants

Data source	Data elements included	Data elements not included	Time period covered
OMB budget data: *Historical Tables* (specifically, *Table 12.3 and other series 12 tables)*	Outlays[a] for grantsto state and local governments "Grants" includes cooperative agreements[b]	Outlays for grants to some nonprofit organizations, for profit institutions, and individuals Outlays for some basic research awarded by competitive grants	1940 through the current budget period

Table 2. (Continued)

Data source	Data elements included	Data elements not included	Time period covered
		(Note: Data for those grants are included in other tables or categories of OMB data, but they are combined with nongrant outlays, so just the grants portion cannot be isolated) Detailed information on recipients Information on the number of individual grant programs	
USASpending.gov	Obligations[c] incurred by federal agencies for grant awards and other types of financial assistance (e.g., loans, cooperative agreements) (Note: Data for grants can be separated from that for other assistance types) Each obligation transaction has associated information including the name of the federal agency making the award, information about the recipient, and CFDA number Recipient information includes type (government, nonprofit or for profit organization, individual); name; and address	Some grant awards less than $25,000[d] Grants awarded by the Legal Services Corporation and the Corporation for Public Broadcasting	Fiscal year 2000 through present
Census Bureau Surveys	Intergovernmental revenue to state and local governments which includes grants, taxes, and loans	Grants to nongovernmentalrecipients	1951 through present

Data source	Data elements included	Data elements not included	Time period covered
	(Note: Data for grants cannot be separated out of the revenue amounts)		

Source: GAO analysis.

[a] Outlay means a payment to liquidate an obligation (other than the repayment of debt principal or other disbursements that are "means of financing" transactions). Outlays generally are equal to cash disbursements, but also are recorded for cash-equivalent transactions, such as the issuance of debentures to pay insurance claims, and in a few cases are recorded on an accrual basis such as interest on public issues of the public debt. Outlays are the measure of government spending.

[b] Cooperative agreements are another form of financial assistance similar to grants, but where the federal agency is more involved with the recipient in implementing the program.

[c] An obligation is a definite commitment that creates a legal liability of the government for payment of goods and services ordered or received. An agency incurs an obligation, for example, when it awards a grant.

[d] OMB's guidance for submitting data to USASpending.gov states that, under the Recovery Act, agencies are required to report all transactions, but can aggregate amounts under $25,000, and that agencies should begin to include aggregate information for all funding types. GSA officials told us agencies are not required by FFATA to include awards under $25,000 related to non-Recovery Act spending.

APPENDIX III: CROSS-CUTTING GRANTS LEGISLATION AND OMB CIRCULARS/AGENCY GRANTS REGULATIONS

Federal grants are typically subject to a wide range of substantive and other requirements under the particular program statutes as well as implementing agency regulations and other guidance that applies to them. They are also governed by many additional cross-cutting requirements that are common to most federal assistance programs.[1]

Figure 6 shows the relevant grant-related public laws that are discussed below.

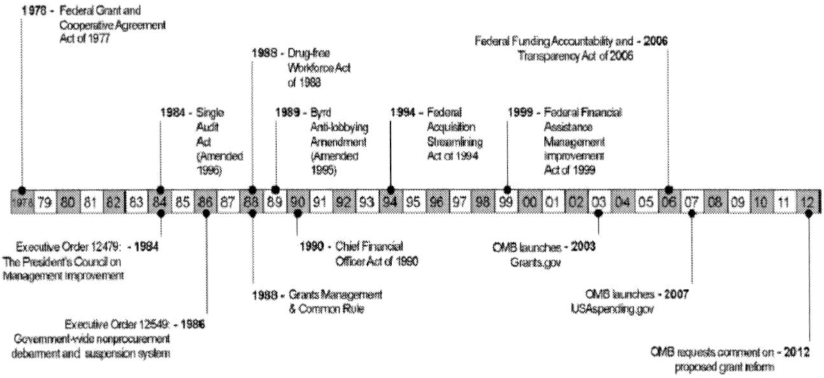

Source: GAO analysis of relevant grant related public laws.

Figure 6. Selected Federal Grants-Related Legislation Timeline.

The Office of Management and Budget (OMB) has long been involved in grants management in the executive branch since its reorganization within the Executive Office of the President in 1970.[2] In 1971, OMB published standards for establishing consistency and uniformity in the administration of grants and other types of financial assistance to state and local governments and certain Indian tribunals.[3] However, even with the publication of OMB's circular for grant administration, the Commission on Government Procurement studying federal spending practices in the early 1970s found that "federal grant-type activities are a vast and complex collection of assistance programs, functioning with little central guidance in a variety of ways that are often inconsistent even for similar programs and projects."[4] The Commission also found that because there were no statutory guidelines for executive agencies to distinguish between assistance relationships, such as grants and procurement relationships with nonfederal entities, agencies were inappropriately using grants to avoid competition and certain requirements that apply to the procurement system.[5] Thereafter, Congress enacted the Federal Grant and Cooperative Agreement Act of 1977[6] to establish standards for executive agencies in selecting the most appropriate funding vehicle. The act directed OMB to provide guidance to executive agencies to promote consistent and efficient use of funding vehicles, and in 1978, OMB issued supplementary interpretive guidelines to help agencies distinguish between assistance programs and procurement relationships.[7]

In 1984, the Administration created the President's Council on Management Improvement, assigning the Deputy Director of OMB as Chairman of the Council.[8] While the Council's role was to review overall management of government programs, several interagency task forces were created under the Council to review various aspects of grants management. Based on recommendations of one task force, the President issued Executive Order No. 12549 in 1986 requiring agencies to participate in a government-wide nonprocurement debarment and suspension system. Thereafter, OMB issued guidelines prescribing the program coverage, government-wide criteria, minimum due process procedures, and other guidance for the system.[9] Another interagency task force explored streamlining the existing guidance for managing federal aid programs, and based on that review, in 1987, the President directed OMB to revise Circular No. A-102, "Grants and Cooperative Agreements with State and Local Governments" to specify uniform, government-wide terms and conditions for grants to state and local governments.[10] The President further directed executive agencies to propose and issue common regulations adopting the terms and conditions set out by OMB verbatim, modified where necessary to reflect inconsistent statutory requirements.[11]

OMB circulars on grants provide policies to be followed by the grant-making agencies, not the grantees. Therefore, prior to the publication of the first grants management common rule in 1988, executive agencies themselves issued regulations to govern their own grant requirements for grantees. Subsequently, each grant-making agency issued four common rules for grants: two are modeled after OMB's grants management circulars covering cost principles, administrative requirements, and audit; a third common rule deals with the prohibition on using grant funds to lobby; and a fourth common rule covers suspension and debarment[12] and drug-free workplace requirements. The federal grant-making agencies' common rules are largely identical regulations that are binding on their grantees.

There were several grant-related laws enacted during the 1980s that focused on promoting accountability and transparency, and preventing abuse, within federal assistance programs. The Single Audit Act, as amended,[13] provides uniform requirements for annual audits of nonfederal entities that expend more than $500,000 in federal awards annually. Prior to this act's enactment, there were no uniform audit requirements for state and local government grantees, and these grantees were often subject to overlapping and conflicting audit requirements associated with each of the assistance programs in which they participated. Congress enacted other federal statutory provisions applicable to all recipients of federal funds, including the prohibition against lobbying with grant funds under the "Byrd Amendment"[14] and the requirement to maintain a drug-free workplace as a precondition of receiving grant funding.[15] Subsequent to the enactment of each of these acts, OMB issued guidance for agencies to implement the requirements of the acts.[16]

One of the key efforts to make government operations more efficient and effective and to prevent waste, fraud, abuse, and financial mismanagement came with the passage of the Chief Financial Officers Act of 1990.[17] The act builds off other legislative initiatives, such as the Single Audit Act, to improve financial management practices in the federal government.[18] The Chief Financial Officers Act created within OMB the Office of Federal Financial Management with specific statutory responsibility for financial management policy, including grants management, for the federal government.[19] While OMB had long taken the lead role in financial management, no entity had been statutorily vested with the responsibility to coordinate financial management practices in the federal government.

Along with the executive branch's efforts to streamline and simplify grants management in the 1980s and 1990s, Congress enacted the Federal Financial Assistance Management Improvement Act of 1999, commonly known as "Public Law 106-107," which required each federal grant-making agency to develop and implement a plan that simplifies the application, administration, and reporting procedures for financial assistance programs. [20] OMB was directed to coordinate this effort by coming up with a common application and reporting system. Following Public Law 106-107 and the President's announcement of the E-government initiative in his 2002 Fiscal Year Management Agenda, OMB established Grants.gov as a central storehouse for information on thousands of grant. To further improve transparency and provide the public with information on federal spending, Congress enacted the Federal Funding Accountability and Transparency Act of 2006.[21] The Act directed OMB to ensure the existence and operation of a single searchable website to be used by the public that shows the name of the entity receiving a federal award, the amount of the award, information on the award, and other information.[22] OMB launched USAspending.gov in 2007 to fulfill the Act's requirements.

The executive branch's recent efforts focus on streamlining administrative requirements and improving the effectiveness of single audits. In furtherance of Public Law 106-107's requirements (discussed above), OMB consolidated its grants-related circulars[23] as well as the agency common rules into Title 2 of the Code of Federal Regulations. Currently, OMB is in the process of re-issuing guidance for each of the common rules under Title 2, allowing federal grant-making agencies to simply adopt the regulations and thereby create a central point for all grantees to locate all grant government-wide requirements.

Concurrent to the streamlining effort, OMB is also working with other stakeholders to evaluate potential reforms in federal grant policies.[24] In an effort to reduce improper payments, OMB created the Single Audit Workgroup with federal and state members who studied a variety of options for improving the effectiveness of single audits. In February 2012, OMB published an advanced notice of proposed guidance detailing a series of reform ideas that would standardize information collection across agencies, adopt a risk-based model for single audits, and provide new administrative approaches for determining and monitoring the allocation of federal funds.[25] The comment period closed at the end of March 2012; OMB has not yet issued proposed guidance based on comments received.

Until the fall of 2011, OMB coordinated grants management policy through two federal boards: the Grants Policy Committee, which was established in 1999, and the Grants Executive Board, which was established in 2004. The Grants Executive Board oversaw the implementation work groups and the Grants.gov initiative while the Grants Policy Committee was composed of grants policy experts from across the federal government whose mission it was to simplify and streamline grant administration policies. In October 2011, OMB announced the creation of the Council on Financial Assistance Reform (COFAR) which replaced these two federal grant bodies. The COFAR is charged with identifying emerging issues, challenges, and opportunities in grants management and policy and providing recommendations to OMB on policies and actions to improve grants administration. According to OMB officials, the COFAR is also expected to serve as a clearinghouse of information on innovations and best practices in grants management. In contrast to the Grants Policy Committee and the Grants Executive Board, which together included members from 26 agencies, the COFAR is made up of the OMB Controller, representatives from the largest eight grant-making agencies, and a representative from one of the smaller federal grant-making agencies. The latter serves a rotating two-year term. Also unlike the Grants Policy Committee, which largely consisted of program level grants staff, the membership of the COFAR is at a higher level, being made up of the Chief Financial Officers of participating agencies. OMB officials told us that the COFAR is now working toward identifying priorities in grants management that may include various initiatives that were started by the defunct Grants Policy Committee and Grants Executive Board. Details on these have yet to be decided.

End Notes

[1] See Office of Management and Budget, *Fiscal Year 2013, Historical Tables, Budget of the U.S. Government.* Specifically, Table 12.3, Federal Outlays for Grants to State and Local Governments, by Function, Agency, and Program: 1940–2013.

[2] GAO, *A Glossary of Terms Used in the Federal Budget Process,* GAO-05-734SP (Washington, D.C.: September 2005) and "Chapter 10, Federal Assistance: Grants and Cooperative Agreements" in GAO, *Principles of Federal Appropriations Law,* Third Edition, Volume II, GAO-06-382SP (February 2006).

[3] For example, some block grants have characteristics normally associated with categorical grants. This type of variation in the characteristics of specific block grants explains why there is some disagreement concerning precisely what constitutes a block grant and how many of them exist.

[4] Constant dollar amounts reflect adjustments for inflation (e.g., the purchasing power of the $91 billion spent in 1980 represents about $221 billion in fiscal year 2011 dollars).

[5] Another way to understand federal grant outlays during this period is to consider them as a percentage of the nation's GDP. Federal grants to state and local governments were equivalent to 3.4 percent of GDP in 1980 and 4.1 percent of GDP in 2011. While this figure has fluctuated somewhat over the last 30 years, it has not demonstrated the dramatic growth seen in federal grant outlays when viewed in constant dollar terms that is shown in figure 3.

[6] GAO, *Block Grants: Characteristics, Experience, and Lessons Learned*, GAO/HEHS-95-74 (Washington, D.C.: Feb. 9, 1995).

[7] The government function grant program categories do not necessarily overlap with program groupings by grant-making agency.

[8] As another example of different methodologies, ACIR included in its counts all direct cash grants to state or local governmental units, other public bodies established under state or local law, or their designee; payments for grants-in-kind, such as purchases of commodities distributed to state or local governmental institutions; payments to nongovernmental entities when such payments result in cash or in-kind services or products that are passed on to state or local governments; payments to state and local governments for research and development that is an integral part of their provision of services; and payments to regional commissions and organizations that are redistributed at the state or local level to provide public services. In contrast, OMB counted only those federal grants for traditional governmental operations, as defined in OMB Circular A-11. The definition covered only grants that "support state or local programs of government operations or provision of services to the public." Accordingly, it excluded federal grants that went directly to individuals, fellowships, most grants to nongovernmental entities, and technical research grants.

[9] As of the end of May 2012, the CFDA listed a total of 2,240 federal assistance programs, including 239 items under a search for formula grants and 1,530 items under a search for project grants. CFDA data are available on the Web at http://www.CFDA.gov.

[10] GAO, *Grants Management: Enhancing Performance Accountability Provisions Could Lead to Better Results,* GAO-06-1046 (Washington, D.C.: Sept. 29, 2006).

[11] GAO, *Agencies' Annual Performance Plans under the Results Act: An Assessment Guide to Facilitate Congressional Decisionmaking*, GAO/GGD/AIMD-10.1.18 (Washington, D.C.: February 1998); and *The Results Act: An Evaluator's Guide to Assessing Agency Annual Performance Plans,* GAO/GGD-10.1.20 (Washington, D.C.: April 1998).

[12] GAO, *Recovery Act: Department of Justice Could Better Assess Justice Assistance Grant Program Impact*, GAO-11-87 (Washington, D.C.: Oct. 15, 2010).

[13] GAO, *Homeland Security: DHS Needs Better Project Information and Coordination among Four Overlapping Grant Programs*, GAO-12-303 (Washington, D.C.: Feb. 28, 2012).

[14] GAO, *Green Building: Federal Initiatives for the Nonfederal Sector Could Benefit from More Interagency Collaboration*, GAO-12-79 (Washington, D.C.: Nov. 2, 2011).

[15] GAO-11-379.

[16] GAO, *2012 Annual Report: Opportunities to Reduce Duplication, Overlap and Fragmentation, Achieve Savings, and Enhance Revenue*, GAO-12-342SP (Washington, D.C.: Feb. 28, 2012).

[17] GAO-12-342SP.

[18] GAO, *Justice Grant Programs: DOJ Should Do More to Reduce the Risk of Unnecessary Duplication and Enhance Program Assessment*, GAO-12-517 (Washington, D.C.: July 12, 2012).

[19] For the purpose of this report we use the term "collaboration" broadly to include interagency activities that others have variously defined as "coordination," "cooperation," "integration," or "networking." We have done so since there are no commonly accepted definitions for these terms and we are unable to make definitive distinctions between these different types of interagency activities. See GAO, *Results Oriented Government: Practices That Can Help Enhance and Sustain Collaboration among Federal Agencies,* GAO-06-15 (Washington, D.C.: Oct. 21, 2005). Here, we use this definition to describe collaboration among intergovernmental participants as well as between nongovernmental grant stakeholders.

[20] Examples of key practices for collaboration include establishing mutually reinforcing or joint strategies, and establishing compatible policies, procedures, and other means of operating across agency boundaries. For additional details, see GAO-06-15.

[21] GAO, *Disaster Assistance: Greater Coordination and an Evaluation of Programs' Outcomes Could Improve Disaster Case Management*, GAO-09-561, (Washington, D.C.: July 8, 2009).

[22] GAO-09-561.

[23] GAO, *Transportation-Disadvantaged Populations: Federal Coordination Efforts Could Be Further Strengthened*, GAO-12-647, (Washington, D.C.: June 20, 2012).

[24] Some federal programs, such as those administered by Veterans Affairs, may provide direct transportation services to beneficiaries, as opposed to funds to state and local agencies to provide these services.

[25] GAO, *Transportation-Disadvantaged Populations: Some Coordination Efforts Among Programs Providing Transportation Services, but Obstacles Persist*, GAO-03-697 (Washington, D.C.: June 30, 2003).

[26] GAO, *Opportunities to Reduce Potential Duplication in Government Programs, Save Tax Dollars, and Enhance Revenue,* GAO-11-318SP (Washington, D.C.: Mar. 1, 2011)

[27] NARA/OIG Audit Report No. 11-03, *Audit of NARA's Oversight of Selected Grantees' Use of Grant Funds*, Feb. 16, 2011.

[28] A subrecipient is an entity that receives a grant award from the prime recipient of an award and is accountable to the prime recipient for the use of the federal funds provided by the subaward.

[29] GAO, *Recovery Act: Energy Efficiency and Conservation Block Grant Recipients Face Challenges Meeting Legislative and Program Goals and Requirements*, GAO-11-379 (Washington, D.C.: Apr. 7, 2011).

[30] GAO, *Medicaid: Federal Oversight of Payments and Program Integrity Needs Improvement,* GAO-12-674T (Washington, D.C.: Apr. 25, 2012).

[31] GAO, *Grants Management: Action Needed to Improve the Timeliness of Grant Closeouts by Federal Agencies,* GAO-12-360 (Washington, D.C.: Apr. 16, 2012).

[32] GAO-12-360.

[33] GAO, *Improper Payments: Remaining Challenges and Strategies for Government-wide Reduction Efforts*, GAO-12-573T (Washington, D.C.: Mar. 28, 2012).

[34] The *2011 Financial Report of the United States Government* includes our report and was issued by the Department of the Treasury on December 23, 2011, and is available through GAO's website at http://www.gao.gov/financial.html and Treasury's website at http://www.fms.treas.gov/fr/index.html.

[35] A deficiency is categorized as a material weakness or a significant deficiency. A material weakness is a deficiency, or combination of deficiencies, in internal control over financial reporting such that there is a reasonable possibility that a material misstatement of the entity's financial statements will not be prevented or detected and corrected on a timely basis. A significant deficiency is less severe than a material weakness, yet important enough to merit attention by those charged with governance.

[36] GAO, *School Improvement Grants: Education Should Take Additional Steps to Enhance Accountability for Schools and Contractors,* GAO-12-373 (Washington, D.C.: Apr.11, 2012).

[37] GAO, *Disaster Recovery: FEMA's Public Assistance Grant Program Experienced Challenges with Gulf Coast Rebuilding*, GAO-09-129 (Washington, D.C.: Dec. 18, 2008).

[38] GAO, *Nonprofit Sector: Treatment and Reimbursement of Indirect Costs Vary among Grants, and Depend Significantly on Federal, State, and Local Government Practices,* GAO-10-477 (Washington, D.C.: May 18, 2010).

End Note for Appendix I

[1] The CFDA can be downloaded in a printable version. We used the online version (CFDA.gov) so we could conduct various searches more easily.

End Notes for Appendix II

[1] The General Services Administration now oversees and administers USASpending.gov.

[2] CRS, *The Federal Funding Accountability and Transparency Act: Background, Overview, and Implementation Issues*. RL33680 (Washington, D.C.: Jan. 31, 2008).

[3] OMB Memorandum M-09-19, *Guidance on Data Submission under the Federal Funding Accountability and Transparency Act (FFATA)* (Washington, D.C.: June 1, 2009).

[4] 13 U.S.C. § 161.

End Notes for Appendix III

[1] We focus this discussion on the history and current status of government-wide grants management. While we focus exclusively on grants, many of the legal requirements and guidance discussed also apply to other forms of federal assistance.

[2] OMB was previously the Bureau of the Budget, which was established within the Department of the Treasury in 1921 but transferred to the Executive Office of the President in 1939.

[3] The first Circular was A-102, "Uniform Administrative Requirements for Grants-In-Aid to State and Local Governments." In 1976, OMB published Circular No. A-110, "Grants and Agreements with Institutions of Higher Education, Hospitals and Other Nonprofit Organizations." 41 Fed. Reg. 32,016 (July 30, 1976).

[4] See S. Rep. No. 95-449 (Sept. 27, 1977), citing The Report of the Commission on Government Procurement, Vol. I, pp. VII-VIII, December 1972.

[5] S. Rep. No. 95-449.

[6] Pub. L. No. 95-224, 92 Stat. 3 (Feb. 3, 1978), *codified, as amended, at* 31 U.S.C. §§ 6301-6308. The act directs executive agencies to use grant agreements or cooperative agreements when the principal purpose of the relationship between the Federal government and the nonfederal entity is to transfer a thing of value to the nonfederal entity to carry out a public purpose of support or stimulation. The law further states that "substantial involvement is not expected between the executive agency and the [grantee] when carrying out the activity contemplated in the agreement." Substantial involvement refers to performance of the funded activity rather than oversight of the grant use.

[7] 43 Fed. Reg. 36,860 (Aug. 18, 1978).

[8] Executive Order 12479, Management Reform in the Federal Government, 49 Fed. Reg. 22,243 (May 29, 1984).

[9] 52 Fed. Reg. 20,360 (May 29, 1987). Executive Order No. 12689, (54 Fed. Reg. 34,131 (Aug. 18, 1989)) and section 2455 of the Federal Acquisition Streamlining Act of 1994, (Pub. L. No. 103-355), established government-wide effect for debarment, suspension, or other exclusions for participants in both procurement and nonprocurement activities.

[10] See 53 Fed. Reg. 8028 (Mar. 11, 1988) (OMB final revisions to Circular No. A-102).

[11] *Memorandum on Grants to State and Local Governments*, President Ronald Reagan (March 12, 1987).

[12] In Executive Order No. 12549 (51 Fed. Reg. 6370 (Feb. 21, 1986)), the President directed the establishment of a common system for debarment and suspension for assistance programs.

[13] 31 U.S.C. §§ 7501-7507. The Single Audit Act was enacted in 1982, and substantially amended in 1996. OMB's implementing guidance is contained in Circular No. A-133, *Audits of States, Local Governments, and Non-Profit Organizations.*

[14] 31 U.S.C § 1352.

[15] Drug-Free Workplace Act of 1988, Pub. L. No. 100-690, Title V, Subtitle D, § 5153, 102 Stat. 4181 (Nov. 18,1988), codified at 41 U.S.C. § 8103.

[16] Both the Single Audit Act of 1984 (Pub. L. No. 98-502) and the Byrd Amendment (Section 319 of Pub. L. No. 101-121), included a requirement OMB to issue guidance for the agency implementation of, and compliance with, the requirements of the act.

[17] Pub. L. No. 101-576, 104 Stat. 2838 (Nov. 15, 1990).

[18] See H.R. Rep. No. 101-818(I) (Oct. 6, 1990).

[19] 31 U.S.C. § 504.

[20] Pub. L. No. 106-107, 113 Stat. 1486 (Nov. 20, 1999).

[21] Pub. L. No. 109-282, 120 Stat. 1186 (Sept. 26, 2006).

[22] Currently pending before Congress is a bill that would expand the scope of spending transparency currently required under the Federal Funding Accountability and Transparency Act of 2006. Among other things, the Digital Accountability and Transparency Act of 2012 (DATA Act), H.R. 2146, 112th Cong. (2012) would establish a new Federal Accountability and Spending Transparency Board charged with collecting spending information and publishing that information in formats that make it easy to search, sort, and download, thus removing OMB's responsibility over spending transparency.

[23] There are currently a total of six OMB circulars on grants, but only three apply to any one type of grantee. Grantees are grouped by (1) states, local governments, and Indian tribes, (2) educational institutions, and (3) nonprofit organizations. OMB published three different circulars on cost principles for each group, published two circulars on administrative requirements (one for states, local governments, and Indian tribes and another for educational institutions and nonprofit organizations combined), and one circular on audit requirements covering all three groups. Circular No. A-133, covering audit requirements, has not been codified into Title 2.

[24] See Exec. Order No. 13520, Reducing Improper Payments and Eliminating Waste in Federal Programs, 74 Fed. Reg. 62,201 (Nov. 25, 2009).

[25] Reform of Federal Policies Relating to Grants and Cooperative Agreements: Cost Principles and Administrative Requirements (including Single Audit Act), Advance Notice of Proposed Guidance, 77 Fed. Reg. 11,778 (Feb. 28, 2012).

In: Federal Grants to State and Local Governments ISBN: 978-1-62417-293-9
Editor: Andrew E. Fisher © 2013 Nova Science Publishers, Inc.

Chapter 2

FEDERAL GRANTS-IN-AID: AN HISTORICAL PERSPECTIVE ON CONTEMPORARY ISSUES*

Robert Jay Dilger

SUMMARY

The federal government is expected to provide state and local governments more than $612 billion in federal grant-in-aid funding in FY2012, encompassing a wide range of public policies, such as health care, transportation, income security, education, job training, social services, community development, and environmental protection. The central role of federal grants-in-aid in American domestic policy was demonstrated by the prominent role grants-in-aid had in the American Recovery and Reinvestment Act of 2009 (ARRA; P.L. 111-5). ARRA is expected to provide state and local governments about $300 billion in federal grants through 2019.

Congress has a central role in determining the scope and nature of federal grant-in-aid programs. In its legislative capacity, Congress first determines what it wants to accomplish and then decides whether a grant-in-aid program is the best means to achieve it. Congress then selects which of the six grant mechanisms to use (project categorical grant, formula categorical grant, formula-project categorical grant, open-end reimbursement categorical grant, block grant, or general revenue sharing), and crafts legislation to accomplish its purpose, incorporating

* This is an edited, reformatted and augmented version of Congressional Research Service, Publication No. R40638, dated March 9, 2012.

the chosen grant instrument. As with all legislated programs generally, Congress oversees the program's implementation to ensure that the federal administrating agency is held accountable for making certain that congressional expectations concerning program performance are met.

Federalism scholars agree that congressional decisions concerning the scope and nature of federal grant-in-aid programs are influenced by both internal and external factors. Internal factors include congressional party leadership and congressional procedures; the decentralized nature of the committee system; the backgrounds, personalities, and ideological preferences of individual Members; and the customs and traditions (norms) that govern congressional behavior. Major external factors include input provided by voter constituencies, organized interest groups, the President, and executive branch officials. Although not directly involved in the legislative process, the Supreme Court, through its rulings on federalism issues, also influences congressional decisions concerning federal grant-in-aid programs.

Overarching all of these factors is the evolving nature of cultural norms and expectations concerning government's role in American society. Over time, the American public has become increasingly accepting of government activism in domestic affairs generally, and of federal government activism in particular. Federalism scholars attribute this increased acceptance of, and sometimes demand for, government action as a reaction to the industrialization and urbanization of American society, technological innovations in communications which have raised awareness of societal problems, and exponential growth in economic interdependencies brought about by an increasingly global economy.

This report provides an historical synopsis of the evolving nature of federal grant-in-aid programs, focusing on the role Congress has played in defining the scope and nature of those programs. It begins with an overview of contemporary federal grant-in-aid programs and then examines their evolution over time, focusing on the internal and external factors that have influenced congressional decisions concerning federal grant-in-aid programs. It concludes with an assessment of the scope and nature of the contemporary federal grants-in-aid system and raises several issues for congressional consideration, including possible ways to augment congressional capacity to provide effective oversight of this system.

THE CONGRESSIONAL ROLE

The federal government is expected to provide state and local governments more than $612 billion in federal grant-in-aid funding in FY2012, encompassing a wide range of public policy areas, such as health care, transportation, income security, education, job training, social services, community development, and environmental protection. The central role of federal grants-in-aid in American domestic policy was demonstrated by the prominent role grants-in-aid had in the $862 billion American Recovery and Reinvestment Act of 2009 (ARRA; P.L. 111-5).[1] ARRA is expected to provide state and local governments about $300 billion in federal grants through 2019.[2]

Congress has a central role in determining the scope and nature of federal grant-in-aid programs. In its legislative capacity, Congress first determines what it wants to accomplish and then decides whether a grant-in-aid program is the best means to achieve it. Congress then selects which of the six grant mechanisms to use (project categorical grant, formula categorical grant, formula-project categorical grant, open-end reimbursement categorical grant, block grant, or general revenue sharing), and crafts legislation to accomplish its purpose, incorporating the chosen grant instrument.[3] As with all legislation generally, Congress oversees the program's implementation to ensure that the federal administrating agency is held accountable for making certain that congressional expectations concerning program performance are met.

Federalism scholars agree that congressional decisions concerning the scope and nature of federal grant-in-aid programs are influenced by both internal and external factors. Internal factors include congressional party leadership and congressional procedures; the decentralized nature of the committee system; the backgrounds, personalities, and ideological preferences of individual Members (especially those of party leaders and committee and subcommittee chairs and ranking minority members); and the customs and traditions (norms) that govern congressional behavior. Major external factors include input provided by voter constituencies, organized interest groups (especially the National Governors Association, the National League of Cities, U.S. Conference of Mayors, and the National Association of Counties), the President, and executive branch officials.[4] Although not directly involved in the legislative process, the Supreme Court, through its rulings on federalism issues, also influences congressional decisions concerning federal grant-in-aid programs.

Overarching all of these factors is the evolving nature of cultural norms and expectations concerning government's role in American society. Over time, the American public has become increasingly accepting of government activism in domestic affairs generally, and of federal government activism in particular. Federalism scholars attribute this increased acceptance of, and sometimes demand for, government action as a reaction to the industrialization and urbanization of American society; technological innovations in communications, which have raised awareness of societal problems; and exponential growth in economic interdependencies brought about by an increasingly global economy.[5]

This report provides an historical synopsis of the evolving nature of federal grant-in-aid programs, focusing on the role Congress has played in defining the scope and nature of those programs. It begins with an overview of contemporary federal grant-in-aid programs and then examines their evolution over time, focusing on the internal and external factors that have influenced congressional decisions concerning federal grant-in-aid programs. It concludes with an assessment of the scope and nature of contemporary federal grants-in-aid and raises several issues for congressional consideration, including possible ways to augment congressional capacity to provide effective oversight of this system.

CONTEMPORARY FEDERAL GRANT-IN-AID PROGRAMS

Different federal departments and agencies, including the U.S. Census Bureau, the Government Accountability Office, and the U.S. Office of Management and Budget use different definitions of federal grants-in-aid. However, there is agreement on the general characteristics associated with each grant type.

There are three general types of federal grants-in-aid programs: categorical grants, block grants, and general revenue sharing. Categorical grants can be used only for a specifically aided program and usually are limited to narrowly defined activities. Block grants can be used only for a specifically aided set of programs and usually are not limited to narrowly defined activities. General revenue sharing can be used for any purpose not expressly prohibited by federal or state law and is not limited to narrowly defined activities.

There are four types of categorical grants: project categorical grants, formula categorical grants, formula-project categorical grants, and open-end reimbursement categorical grants. Project categorical grants are awarded on a competitive basis through an application process specified by the federal agency making the grant. Formula categorical grants are allocated among recipients according to factors specified within enabling legislation or administrative regulations (e.g., population, median household income, per capita income, poverty, miles driven). Formula-project categorical grants use a mixture of fund allocation means, typically involving the use of a formula specified within enabling legislation or administrative regulations to allocate available funds among the states, followed by an application process specified by each recipient state to allocate available funds on a competitive basis among local governments or other eligible applicants. Open-end reimbursement categorical grants, often regarded as the equivalent of formula categorical grants, provide a reimbursement of a specified proportion of recipient program costs, eliminating competition among recipients as well as the need for an allocation formula.[6]

A Continuum of Federal Grants-in-Aid Administrative Conditions

Of the six grant types, project categorical grants typically impose the most restraint on recipients (see **Table 1**). Federal administrators have a high degree of control over who receives project categorical grants (recipients must apply to the appropriate federal agency for funding and compete against other potential recipients who also meet the program's specified eligibility criteria); recipients have relatively little discretion concerning aided activities (funds must be used for narrowly specified purposes); and there is a relatively high degree of federal administrative conditions attached to the grant, typically involving the imposition of federal standards for planning, project selection, fiscal management, administrative organization, and performance.

General revenue sharing imposes the least restraint on recipients.[7] Federal administrators have a low degree of discretion over who receives general revenue sharing (funding is allocated automatically to recipients by a formula or formulas specified in legislation); recipients have broad discretion concerning aided activities; and there is a relatively low degree of federal administrative conditions attached to the grant, typically involving periodic reporting criteria and the application of standard government accounting procedures.

Block grants are at the midpoint in the continuum of recipient discretion. Federal administrators have a low degree of discretion over who receives block grants (after setting aside funding for administration and other specified activities, the remaining funds are typically allocated automatically to recipients by a formula or formulas specified in legislation); recipients have some discretion concerning aided activities (typically, funds can be used for a specified range of activities within a single functional area); and there is a moderate degree of federal administrative conditions attached to the grant, typically involving more than periodic reporting criteria and the application of standard government accounting procedures, but with fewer conditions attached to the grant than project categorical grants.

Table 1. Classification of Grant Types by Three Defining Traits

Federal Administrator's Funding Discretion		
Low Formula Categorical Grant	Medium Block Grant—Formula-Project Categorical Grant	High Project Categorical Grant
Open-ended Reimbursement Categorical Grant		
General Revenue Sharing		
Range of Recipient's Discretion in Use of Funds		
Low	Medium	High
Project Categorical Grant Formula-Project Categorical Grant	Block Grant	General Revenue Sharing
Formula Categorical Grant		
Open-ended Reimbursement Categorical Grant		
Extent of Performance Conditions		
Low	Medium	High
General Revenue Sharing	Block Grant	Project Categorical Grant Formula Categorical Grant
		Formula-Project Categorical Grant
		Open-ended Reimbursement Categorical Grant

Source: U.S. Advisory Commission on Intergovernmental Relations, *Categorical Grants: Their Role and Design*, A52 (Washington, DC: GPO, 1978), p. 7.

FEDERAL GRANT-IN-AID FUNDING

As indicated in Table 2, federal spending on grants-in-aid to state and local governments has increased over the years, and is expected to reach an historic high of $612.4 billion in FY2012. The recent growth in federal funding to state and local governments is expected to moderate somewhat over the next several fiscal years as ARRA funds are expended, but to remain at historically high levels.

Table 2. Federal Grant-In-Aid Expenditures, by Function, Selected FY1902-FY2012 (nominal $ in millions)

Fiscal Year	Total	Health	Income Security	Education, Training, Employment and Social Services	Transportation	Community and Regional Development	Other
2012(est.)	$612,419	$275,199	$106,151	$114,769	$66,695	$17,662	$31,943
2011	606,766	292,847	113,625	98,147	60,986	19,935	21,226
2010	608,390	290,168	115,156	97,586	60,981	18,818	25,681
2000	285,874	124,843	68,653	36,672	32,222	8,665	14,819
1990	135,325	43,890	36,768	21,780	19,174	4,965	8,748
1980	91,385	15,758	18,495	21,862	13,022	6,486	15,762
1970	24,065	3,849	5,795	6,417	4,599	1,780	1,625
1960	7,019	214	2,635	525	2,999	109	537
1950	2,212	123	1,123	484	429	0	53
1940	967	22	271	238	165	0	271
1930	100	0	1	22	76	0	1
1922	118	0	1	7	92	0	18
1913	12	0	2	3	0	0	7
1902	7	0	1	1	0	0	5

Sources: U.S. Office of Management and Budget, *Budget of the United States Government, Fiscal Year 2013: Historical Tables* (Washington, DC: GPO, 2012), pp. 251-259, http://www.whitehouse.gov/sites/default/files/omb/ budget/fy2013/ assets/hist.pdf; and U.S. Department of Commerce, Bureau of the Census, *Historical Statistics of the United States, Colonial Times to 1970, Part 2* (Washington, DC: GPO, 1975), pp. 1123, 1125, http://www2.census.gov/prod2/ statcomp/documents/ CT1970p2-12.pdf.

ARRA is expected to provide $236 billion in tax cuts and $626 billion in spending from FY2009 through FY2019, including about $300 billion for federal grant-in-aid programs for state and local governments.[8] ARRA provides additional funding for a wide range of federal grant-in-aid programs, such as Medicaid ($93 billion, primarily for a temporary increase in the Federal Medical Assistance Percentages reimbursement rate), a new State Fiscal Stabilization Fund ($53.6 billion), Build America Bonds ($30 billion), Highways and Bridges ($27.5 billion), Title 1-A, elementary and secondary education for the disadvantaged, ($13 billion), Individuals with Disabilities Education Act ($12.2 billion), Public Transit ($8.4 billion), Intercity Passenger

Rail Capital, Congestion, and Corridor Development grants ($8 billion), Temporary Assistance for Needy Families ($5 billion), and Weatherization Assistance Grants ($5 billion).

As indicated in Table 2 and Figure 1, health care accounts for almost half of all federal grant-in-aid funding (an estimated $275.9 billion in FY2012, or 44.9% of total federal grant-in-aid funding), followed by income security ($106.2 billion, or 17.3%), education, training, employment and social services ($114.8 billion, or 18.7%), transportation ($66.7 billion, or 10.9%), and community and regional development ($17.7 billion, or 2.9%).

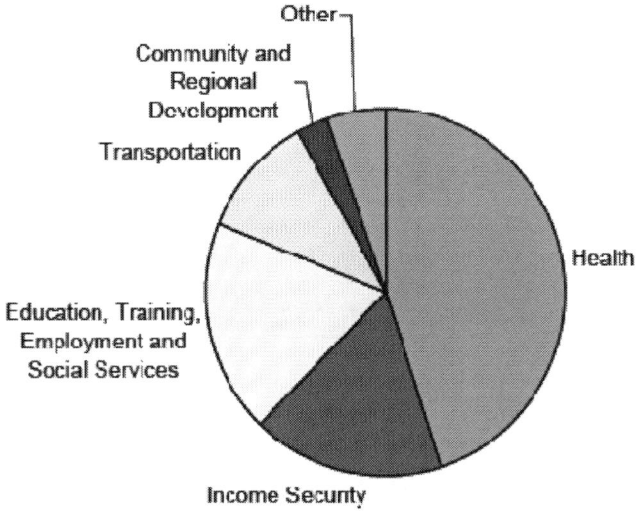

Source: U.S. Office of Management and Budget, *Budget of the United States Government, Fiscal Year 2013: Historical Tables* (Washington, D.C.: GPO, 2012), p. 259, http://www.whitehouse.gov/sites/default/files/omb/budget/fy2013/assets/hist.pdf.

Figure 1. Federal Grant-In-Aid Expenditures, by Function, FY2012 Estimate.

Medicaid, with $255.3 billion in expected outlays in FY2012, has, by far, the largest budget of any federal grant-in-aid program. Eight other programs are expected to have outlays in excess of $9 billion in FY2012: Federal-Aid Highways ($38.6 billion), Accelerating Achievement and Ensuring Equity (Education for the Disadvantaged—$20.1 billion), Child Nutrition ($19.4 billion),[9] Tenant Based Rental Assistance—Section 8 vouchers ($18.2 billion), Temporary Assistance for Needy Families ($16.5 billion), Special Education

($14.3 billion), the Children's Health Insurance Fund ($9.8 billion), and State Children and Families Services Programs ($9.7 billon).

Table 3 provides data on grant-in-aid expenditures in nominal and constant (inflation-adjusted) dollars, as a percentage of federal outlays and as a percentage of gross domestic product for selected years since 1960. It also indicates the percentage of grant-in-aid expenditures that are payments for individuals, as opposed to payments for capital improvements and government operations.

Table 3. Federal Grant-In-Aid Expenditures, Percentage of Expenditures for Individuals, Constant Dollars, and as a Percentage of Federal Outlays and Gross Domestic Product, Selected Fiscal Years, 1960-2012

Fiscal Year	Nominal $ (in millions)	% Expenditures for Individuals	Constant $ (FY2005)	% of Federal Outlays	% of GDP
2012 (est.)	$612,419	60.2%	$504,400	16.1%	3.9%
2011	606,766	63.9%	514,600	16.8%	4.1%
2010	608,390	63.2%	527,100	17.6%	4.2%
2005	428,018	64.0%	428,000	17.3%	3.5%
2000	285,874	63.9%	326,800	16.0%	2.9%
1995	224,991	64.2%	283,600	14.8%	3.1%
1990	135,325	57.1%	198,100	10.8%	2.4%
1985	105,852	47.3%	189,600	11.2%	2.6%
1980	91,385	35.6%	227,100	15.5%	3.4%
1975	49,791	33.6%	186,900	15.0%	3.2%
1970	24,065	36.2%	123,700	12.3%	2.4%
1965	10,910	34.1%	65,900	9.2%	1.6%
1960	7,019	35.3%	45,300	7.6%	1.4%

Source: U.S. Office of Management and Budget, *Budget of the United States Government, Fiscal Year 2013: Historical Tables* (Washington, D.C.: GPO, 2012), pp. 251, 252.

As indicated in **Table 3**, total federal grant-in-aid expenditures has increased since 1960, whether measured in nominal dollars, constant dollars, as a percentage of federal outlays, or as a percentage of gross domestic product. However, the pace of expenditure increases for federal grant-in-aid programs has varied over the years. Federal grant-in-aid expenditures increased, in nominal dollars, 187.3% during the 1960s, 246.4% during the 1970s, 33.4% during the 1980s, 98.0% during the 1990s, and 98.6% during the first decade of the 2000s.[10]

Expenditure growth for federal grant-in-aid programs has, in most years, exceeded inflation. However, as indicated in **Table 3**, grant-in-aid expenditures, expressed in constant (FY2005) dollars, did not keep pace with inflation during the early 1980s.

Federalism scholars have noted that since the 1980s, the focus of federal grant-in-aid programs has shifted from providing assistance to places (e.g., to build public highways, support public education, criminal justice systems, economic development endeavors and government administration) to people (e.g., providing health care benefits, social welfare income, housing assistance, and social services).[11] Much of this shift is attributed to Medicaid, which has experienced relatively large expenditure growth over the past several decades. As shown in **Table 3**, payments for individuals accounted for about one-third of federal grant-in-aid expenditures during the 1960s and 1970s, compared with more than 60% since the mid-1990s.

In the past, the now-defunct U.S. Advisory Commission on Intergovernmental Relations (ACIR) and the U.S. Office of Management and Budget (OMB) used information contained in the Catalog of Federal Domestic Assistance (CFDA) to determine the number of federal grant-in-aid programs. The CFDA "is a government-wide compendium of Federal programs, projects, services, and activities that provide assistance or benefits to the American public."[12] It lists 15 categories of federal grants: formula grants (including formula categorical grants, formula-project categorical grants, and block grants); project grants; direct payments for specified uses to individuals and private firms; direct payments with unrestricted use to beneficiaries who meet federal eligibility requirements; direct loans; guaranteed/insured loans; insurance; sale, exchange, or donation of property and goods; use of property, facilities and equipment; provision of specialized services; advisory services and counseling; dissemination of technical information; training; investigation of complaints; and federal employment. It lists all authorized federal grant programs, including grants that have not received an appropriation. Because the CFDA focuses on the needs of applicants, if a program uses a separate application or other delivery mechanism, the CFDA considers it a separate program. This complicates efforts to count federal grant-in-aid programs. For example, the CFDA lists four entries for the State Fiscal Stabilization Fund.

ACIR published counts of funded federal grant-in-aid programs for FYs 1975, 1978, 1981, 1984, 1987, 1989, 1991, 1993 and 1995.[13] OMB provided counts of funded grants-in-aid programs for FYs 1980-2003.[14] Because they used a different methodology to determine which grant programs to include in their count, their results differed. OMB consistently identified fewer grants than ACIR. For example, in 1995, OMB identified 608 funded federal grant-in-aid programs compared to ACIR's count of 633.[15] No authoritative count of funded federal grant-in-aid programs is known to have been issued in recent years.

ACIR included in its counts all direct cash grants to state or local governmental units, other public bodies established under state or local law, or their designee; payments for grants-in-kind, such as purchases of commodities distributed to state or local governmental institutions; payments to nongovernmental entities when such payments result in cash or in-kind services or products that are passed on to state or local governments; payments to state and local governments for research and development that is an integral part of their provision of services; and payments to regional commissions and organizations that are redistributed at the state or local level to provide public services.[16]

OMB counted only those federal grants for traditional governmental operations, as defined in OMB Circular A-11. The definition covered only grants that "support State or local programs of government operations or provision of services to the public."[17] It excluded federal grants that went directly to individuals, fellowships, most grants to nongovernmental entities, and technical research grants.

A search of the CFDA indicated that state governments, local governments, U.S. territories, and/or federally recognized tribal governments are eligible to apply for 1,263 federal grant-in-aid programs (defined as authorized project grants, formula grants, direct payments for specified uses, and direct payments for unrestricted uses).[18] Of these programs, 135 are not currently funded and 132 are research, fellowship, or exchange programs that are available to both public and private institutions of higher education and are not targeted solely at either public institutions of higher education or other public agencies. Removing them from the list leaves 996 funded federal grants-in-aid programs. Because there is no current consensus on the methodology used to count federal grants-in-aid programs, the 996 count of federal grant-in-aid programs listed in **Table 4** for January 2012 that was compiled from the CFDA should be viewed as illustrative, as opposed to definitive, of the current number of federal grant-in-aid programs for state and local governments.

As the data in the table suggest, the number of grant-in-aid programs to state and local governments increased slowly from 1902 to 1930. Then, partly in reaction to the Great Depression, Congress increased the number of grant-in-aid programs available to state and local governments over the next three decades, roughly doubling the number of grants each decade. During the 1960s, Congress increased the number of federal grants-in-aid exponentially, primarily in response to national social movements concerning poverty and civil rights. Congress continued to increase the number of federal grant-in-aid programs during the 1970s, but at a somewhat slower pace as it addressed budgetary constraints presented by "guns versus butter" issues associated with the Vietnam conflict. The rate of increase slowed further during the 1980s, as Congress addressed budgetary constraints presented by demographic changes in American society that led to escalating costs for several federal entitlement programs, especially for Social Security, Medicare and Medicaid, and to efforts to merge categorical grant programs in several functional areas into block grants. As the data in **Table 4** suggest, Congress continued to increase the number of federal grant-in-aid programs available to state and local governments during the 1990s, and has continued to do so in recent years.

Table 4. Federal Grants-In-Aid, by Type, Selected Years, 1902-2012

Year	# of Grants	Categorical	Block	General Revenue Sharinga
2012	996	968	28b	0
2009	953	928	25b	0
1998	664	640	24	0
1991	557	543	14	0
1980	539	534	4	1
1968	387	385	2	0
1960	132	132	0	0
1952	71	71	0	0
1940	34	34	0	0
1930	15	5	0	0
1920	11	11	0	0
1902	4	4	0	0

Source: CRS computation, U.S. General Services Administration, *The Catalog of Federal Domestic Assistance* (Washington, D.C.: GPO, 2010), https://www.cfda.gov/downloads/CFDA_2010.pdf; U.S. General Services Administration, *The Catalog of Federal Domestic Assistance* on-line edition (January 2011), https://www.cfda.gov/; David B. Walker, *The Rebirth of* Federalism, 2nd Edition (NY: Chatham House Publishers, 2000), pp. 6,7; U.S. Advisory Commission on Intergovernmental Relations (ACIR), *Characteristics of Federal Grant-In-Aid Programs to State and Local Governments : Grants Funded FY 1995* (Washington, D.C.: GPO, 1995), p. 3, and ACIR, *Categorical Grants: Their Role and Design*, A-52 (Washington, D.C.: GPO, 1978), p. 28.

[a] General revenue sharing distributed funds to states from 1972 to 1981 and to localities from 1972 to 1986.

[b] For further analysis, see CRS Report R40486, *Block Grants: Perspectives and Controversies*, by Robert Jay Dilger and Eugene Boyd.

LAND GRANTS AND "DUAL FEDERALISM": 1776-1860

The relative influence of internal versus external factors on congressional decisions affecting federal grant-in-aid programs has varied, both over time and in each specific policy area. Prior to the Civil War, external factors, especially cultural norms and expectations concerning government's role in American society, restricted congressional options concerning enactment of federal grant-in-aid programs for state and local governments.

During this time period, America was primarily a rural nation of farmers. Travel conditions were, compared to today's standards, primitive. Many Americans rarely left their home state, and many others never set foot in another state. Government as we know it today, with regulations and spending programs affecting many aspects of American life, did not exist. Although ratification of the Articles of Confederation and Perpetual Union on March 1, 1781 formally established the United States of America, personal allegiance was still directed more toward the individual's home state than to the nation. It was an era of what federalism scholars have called "dual federalism," where states were expected to be the primary instrument of governance in domestic affairs.[19]

However, even before the Constitution's ratification, the federal government found ways to provide state and local governments assistance to encourage them to pursue national policy objectives. For example, under the Articles of Confederation and Perpetual Union, Congress did not have the power to lay and collect taxes and relied heavily on state donations to fund the government. This lack of revenue, and expenses related to national defense, limited congressional spending options in domestic affairs. The Congress of the Confederation addressed that issue by adopting the Land Ordinance of 1785. The Ordinance generated revenue for the government by authorizing the sale of land acquired from Great Britain at the conclusion of the American Revolutionary War. The Ordinance also required every new township incorporated in those lands, called the Ohio Country, to be subdivided into 36 lots (or sections), each one mile square. Lots 8, 11, 26 and 29 were reserved for the United States.[20] The new townships were required to use Lot 16 "for the maintenance of public schools, within the said township."[21] Some schools are still located in lot 16 of their respective townships, although many of the school lots were sold to raise money for public education. These land grants for public education were reauthorized by Congress in the Northwest Ordinance of 1787.[22] Congress subsequently adopted similar legislation for all states admitted to the union from 1802 to 1910, with exceptions for Texas, which retained all of its public land, and Maine and West Virginia which were formed from other states. From 1802 to 1848, one lot in each township was to be used for education, from 1848 to 1890 two lots, and from 1894 to 1910, with one exception, four lots.[23]

When the Framers met in Philadelphia in 1787 to rework the Articles of Confederation and Perpetual Union, the national economy was in recession, state governments were saddled with large debts left over from the Revolutionary War, the continental dollar was unstable and destined to be a national joke ("not worth a continental"), the navy could not protect international shipping, and the army proved unable to protect its own arsenal during Shay's rebellion in 1786. To address these issues, Congress was provided 17 specific powers in Article 1, Section 8 of the U.S. Constitution, ratified in 1789, including the power to coin money, establish post offices, regulate copyright laws, declare war, regulate the armed forces, borrow money, and, importantly, lay and collect taxes.

The power to lay and collect taxes provided Congress the means to expand the federal government's role in domestic affairs. Moreover, the Supreme Court issued several rulings under Chief Justice John Marshall concerning congressional authority to regulate interstate commerce that effectively cleared the way for congressional activism in domestic policy.[24] However, the prevailing view in Congress at this time was that any power not explicitly provided to Congress in the Constitution was excluded purposively, suggesting that in the absence of specific, supporting constitutional language the exercise of governmental police powers (the regulation of private interests for the protection of public safety, health and morals; the prevention of fraud and oppression; and the promotion of the general welfare) was either meant to be a state or local government responsibility, or outside the scope of governmental authority altogether.

Nevertheless, during the 1800s there were congressional efforts, primarily from representatives from western states, to adopt legislation to provide federal cash assistance for various types of internal improvement projects to encourage western migration and promote interstate commerce. Most of these efforts failed, primarily due to sectional divisions within the Congress which, at that time, made it difficult to build coalitions large enough to adopt programs that targeted most of its assistance to western states; opposition from Members of Congress who viewed reducing the national debt from the American Revolutionary War as a higher priority; and opposition from Members who viewed the provision of cash assistance for internal improvements, other than for post roads which were specifically mentioned in the Constitution as a federal responsibility, a violation of states' rights, as articulated in the Tenth Amendment's language: "The powers not delegated to the United States by the Constitution, nor prohibited by it to the States, are reserved to the States respectively, or to the people."[25]

Given prevailing views concerning the limited nature of the federal government's role in domestic affairs, instead of authorizing direct cash assistance to states for internal improvements, Congress typically authorized federal land grants to states. For example, in 1823 Ohio received a federal land grant of 60,000 acres along the Maumee Road to raise revenue to improve that road. In 1827, Ohio received another federal land grant of 31,596 acres to raise revenue for the Columbus and Sandusky Turnpike.[26]

In 1841, nine states (Ohio, Indiana, Illinois, Alabama, Missouri, Mississippi, Louisiana, Arkansas, and Michigan), and, with three exceptions, all subsequent newly admitted states were designated land grant states and guaranteed at least 500,000 acres of federal land to be auctioned to support transportation projects, including roads, railroads, bridges, canals and improvement of water courses, that expedited the transportation of the United States mail and military personnel and munitions.[27] By 1900, over 3.2 million acres of federal land were donated to these states to support wagon road construction. Congress also authorized the donation of another 4.5 million acres of federal land to Illinois, Indiana, Michigan, Ohio and Wisconsin to raise revenue for canal construction and 2.225 million acres to Alabama, Iowa and Wisconsin to improve river navigation. In addition, states were provided 37.8 million acres for railroad improvements and 64 million acres for flood control.[28] States were provided wide latitude in project selection and federal oversight and administrative regulations were minimal.

Although land grants were prevalent throughout the 1800s, given prevailing views concerning states rights land grants, as well as cash grants, were subject to opposition on constitutional grounds. For example, in 1854, Congress adopted legislation authorizing the donation of 10 million acres of federal land to states to be sold to provide for the indigent insane. President Franklin Pierce vetoed the legislation claiming that

> I cannot find any authority in the Constitution making the federal government the great almoner of public charity throughout the United States. To do so would, in my judgment, be contrary to the letter and spirit of the Constitution, and subversive of the whole theory upon which the union of these States is founded. ... I respectfully submit that, in a constitutional point of view, it is wholly immaterial whether the appropriation be in money, or in land.... should this bill become a law, ...

> the several States instead of bestowing their own means on the social wants of their own people, may themselves ... become humble supplicants for the bounty of the Federal Government, reversing the state's true relation to this Union.[29]

One notable exception to the federal reluctance to provide cash grants to states occurred in 1837. The federal government used proceeds from western land sales to retire the federal debt in 1836. The Deposit Act of 1836 directed that, after reserving $5 million, any money in the federal Treasury on January 1, 1837 shall be distributed to states in proportion to their respective representation in the House and Senate. There were no restrictions placed on how states were to use the funds. About $30 million was distributed to states in three quarterly payments in 1837 before the banking crisis of 1837 led to a recession and payments were stopped. To avoid a promised veto from President Andrew Jackson, the legislation indicated that the funds were a deposit subject to recall, rather than an outright grant of cash.[30]

Overall, domestic policy in the United States prior to the Civil War was dominated by states. As a federalism scholar put it:

> With respect to the classic trinity of sovereign powers – taxation, the police power, and eminent domain – the states enjoyed broad autonomous authority, which they exercised vigorously. Indeed, property law, commercial law, corporation law, and many other aspects of law vital to the economy were left almost exclusively to the states.... Federalism thus provided a receptive structure for expressions of state autonomy and pursuit of state-oriented economic objectives, not only as a matter of constitutional theory and the distribution of formal authority but also as a matter of real power.[31]

THE ORIGINS OF THE MODERN GRANTS-IN-AID SYSTEM: 1860-1932

The Union's victory in the Civil War marked the beginning of a second evolutionary era in American federalism. It effectively put to an end to the doctrine that the Constitution was a compact among sovereign states, each with the right to nullify an act of Congress that the state deemed unconstitutional, and each with the legal right to secede from the Union.[32] It also signaled the triumph of the northern states' commercialism over the southern states' agrarianism:

> Unimpeded by the political opposition of the southern slavocracy, the Republican coalition of north and west carried through a program of comprehensive changes that insured the expansion of industry, commerce, and free farming.... Instead of the policies of economic laissez faire that the slavocracy had demanded ... the Republicans substituted the doctrine that the federal government would provide assistance for business, industry, and farming; the protective tariff, homestead, land subsidies for agricultural colleges, transcontinental railroads and other internal improvements, national banks. When the defeated south came back into the Union, it had to accept the comprehensive alternation in government policy and economic institutions that historian Charles A. Beard was later to name the Second American Revolution.[33]

Following the war, three constitutional amendments - the Thirteenth adopted in 1865, the Fourteenth adopted in 1868, and the Fifteenth Amendment adopted in 1870 - abolished slavery, prohibited states from denying due process or equal protection to any of their citizens, and banned racial restrictions on voting, respectively. In addition, Congress enacted the Reconstruction Acts of 1867 and 1868, which imposed military government on the formally secessionist states and required universal manhood suffrage.[34] Despite this active federal presence in domestic policy in the South following the Civil War, the concept of dual federalism and deference to states in domestic affairs remained a part of American culture. For example, several Supreme Court rulings during this time period limited congressional efforts to override state laws on civil rights, in effect leaving civil and voting rights matters to states until the 1950s and 1960s.[35] The Supreme Court also limited congressional efforts to regulate interstate commerce by limiting the Interstate Commerce Commission's authority.[36]

Reflecting prevailing views concerning dual federalism, and limited federal fiscal resources, the first annual cash grant to states, other than for the support of the National Guard, was not adopted until 1887. The Hatch Act of 1887 provided each state an annual cash grant of $15,000 to establish agricultural experiment stations. It marked the beginning of the modern grants-in-aid system. In 1888, an annual grant of $25,000 was appropriated for the care of disabled veterans in state hospitals. States were provided $100 per disabled veteran.[37] In 1890, funding was provided to subsidize resident instruction in the land grant colleges made possible by the Morrill Act of 1862, which provided each existing and future state with 60,000 acres of federal land, plus an additional 30,000 acres for each of its congressional representatives, to be sold for the endowment, support, and maintenance of at least one college where the leading subject was agriculture and the mechanic arts.[38]

In 1902, there were four annual grants-in-aid programs in operation (funding for the National Guard, agricultural experiment stations, the care of disabled veterans, and resident instruction in the land grant colleges), accounting for about $7 million or about 1% of federal expenditures. State and local government expenditures at that time were slightly over $1 billion, evidence of the relatively limited nature of federal involvement in domestic policy at that time.

An important difference between land grants and grants-in-aid had emerged, even at this early date. Because grants-in-aid were funded from the federal treasury, many in Congress felt that they had an obligation to ensure that the funds were spent by states in an appropriate manner. As a result, Congress began to attach an increasing number of administrative requirements to these grant programs. For example, in 1889, states were required to match federal funding for the care of disabled veterans or lose it. The Morrill Act of 1890 authorized the Secretary of the Interior to withhold payments, pending an appeal to Congress, from states that failed to meet conditions specified in the act. In 1895, expenditures authorized by the Hatch Act for agricultural experiment stations were conditioned by annual audits. In 1911, funding authorized by the Weeks Act to support state efforts to prevent forest fires were conditioned by advance approval of state plans for the funds' use, annual audits and inspections, and a state matching requirement.[39]

The Sixteenth Amendment's ratification in 1913 provided Congress the authority to lay and collect taxes on income. Although the federal income tax initially generated only modest amounts, it provided Congress an opportunity to shift from land grants to grants-in-aid to encourage state and local governments to provide additional attention to policy areas Congress considered of national interest. Between 1913 and 1923, Congress adopted new grant-in-aid programs for highway construction, vocational education, public health, and maternity care. Federal spending on grants-in-aid increased from $12 million in 1913 to $118 million in 1922.

In 1923, Massachusetts brought suit against the Secretary of the Treasury, Andrew Mellon, claiming that the maternal care grants authorized by the Sheppard-Towner Act of 1921 were unconstitutional infringements on states' rights. The Supreme Court dismissed the case on the grounds that it lacked jurisdiction. Nonetheless, Justice George Sutherland, writing on behalf of the unanimous Court, indicated that, in his view, this form of congressional spending was not unconstitutional because grants-in-aid were optional and, as such, were not coercive instruments.[40] As a result, although few new grant-in-aid programs were adopted during the remainder of the 1920s, grants-in-aid were now accepted as a legal means for Congress to encourage state and local governments to pursue national goals.

THE NEW DEAL AND THE RISE OF "COOPERATIVE FEDERALISM": 1932-1960

Political scientists contend that about once in every generation partisan affiliations realign across the nation, typically taking a few years to materialize but often becoming apparent during a "critical" presidential election. Critical elections typically result in relatively dramatic and lasting changes in the partisan composition within Congress and state governments. They also usually signal the coming to power of a new partisan coalition that dominates congressional decision-making for a relatively long period of time. For example, the election of 1896 ended the political stalemate between the Democratic and Republican parties and solidified the Republican Party's position as the majority party for the next 36 years. The election of 1932 signaled a new period of Democratic Party dominance, particularly in the "Solid South," that lasted until the 1970s when partisan attachments began to weaken, southern states became increasing Republican, and the two major political parties became increasingly competitive, each seemingly on the verge of achieving majority party status at various times, but unable to retain that status permanently.[41]

The 1932-1960 time period also saw the emergence of the "congressional conservative coalition," the unofficial title given to the shifting political alliances of southern, conservative Democrats and Republican Members. The conservative coalition became an increasingly important counterbalance to large Democratic majorities in both houses of Congress. Members of the conservative coalition generally advocated balanced budgets and states rights, especially in civil rights legislation. They used congressional procedures, such as the filibuster or threat of a filibuster, to win concessions from the Democratic majority, and, in some instances, to prevent legislation they opposed from becoming law. They also benefitted from the congressional seniority system, which, during this time period, allocated committee chairmanships according to seniority. Because many of the congressional districts in the "solid south" were non-competitive seats, southern representatives held a disproportionate number of committee chairmanships in the House, further strengthening the conservative coalition's influence on congressional policymaking.

The conservative coalition prevented civil rights legislation from being enacted during this time period, but it could not prevent Democratic majorities in the House and Senate from expanding the federal government's presence in domestic policy. However, throughout this time period, the conservative coalition actively sought concessions to ensure that any new federal programs, including any new federal grant-in-aid programs, respected state rights. As a result, the grant-in-aid programs adopted during this time period tended to be in policy areas where state and local governments were already active, such as in education, health care, and highway construction, or where additional federal assistance was welcomed, such as job creation. Also, federal administrative conditions attached to grant-in-aid programs during this era focused on the prevention of corruption and fraudulent expenditures as opposed to encouraging states to move in new policy directions. As a result, federalism scholars have labeled this time period as an era of "cooperative federalism," where intergovernmental tensions were relatively minor and state and local governments were provided flexibility in project selection.

Faced with unprecedented national unemployment and economic hardship, President Franklin Delano Roosevelt advocated during his presidency a dramatic expansion of the federal government's role in domestic affairs, including an expansion of grants-in-aid as a means to help states combat poverty and create jobs. Congress approved 16 new, continuing grant-in-aid programs during the years 1933-1938, and increased funding for continuing federal grant-in-aid programs from $214 million in 1932 to $790 million in 1938.[42]

Congress also enacted several temporary, emergency relief grant-in-aid programs that distributed federal funds to states according to the state's fiscal capacity. Congress devised mathematical formulas, based on a variety of economic and business measures, to allocate funding to each state, resulting in the share of relief funds varying among states based on the formula's assessment of need. At their peak, in 1935, emergency relief measures provided states nearly $1.9 billion to create jobs and provide emergency assistance for the unemployed. The emergency relief programs were terminated during the 1940s, but they established a precedent for extensive federal involvement with state and local governments in areas of national concern and for the use of mathematical formulas for distributing federal assistance.[43]

The Social Security Act of 1935 (SSA) was, arguably, the most significant legislative enactment of the New Deal period. It established a federal presence in social welfare policy. New grant-in-aid programs were established for old age assistance, aid to the blind, aid to dependent children, unemployment compensation, maternal and child health, crippled children, and child welfare. Also, federal oversight of grant-in-aid spending was enhanced as auditing requirements were now required in almost all grant programs. Also, in 1939, state employees administering SSA programs were required to be selected by merit system procedures, a major advancement for the development of professional state and local government administration and a signal of the declining influence of state and local party bosses in American society. In 1940, the Hatch Act restricted the political activities of state and local government employees paid with federal funds.[44]

Legally, New Deal legislation was based on an expanded interpretation of congressional authority to spend through grant-in-aid programs to promote the nation's welfare under Article 1, Section 8, clause 1 of the Constitution, often referred to as the congressional "spending power." Federal expenditures through grant-in-aid programs during the New Deal were made in several functional areas, including some, such as social welfare, that were traditionally viewed as state responsibilities. Opponents of an expanded role for the federal government in domestic policy argued that New Deal grant programs precluded state action in these traditionally state functional areas and, as such, violated the Constitution's Tenth Amendment. Advocates of an expansion of federal involvement in domestic affairs argued that the power of Congress to spend is more extensive than, rather than concurrent with, enumerated or even implied law-making powers. This disagreement led to a number of Supreme Court cases, a full discussion of which is beyond the scope of this report. The Supreme Court rejected the New Deal's expansion of federal authority in eight of the first ten cases that it decided. Then, after President Roosevelt's failed legislative proposal to "pack the Court" in 1937, the Supreme Court upheld the constitutionality of several New Deal laws, including the Social Security Act.[45] As one federalism scholar noted:

> A new era of judicial construction had been launched. The commerce power was given broad interpretation in cases upholding the Labor Relations Act. The older distinction between direct and indirect effects of commercial activity was abandoned and the more realistic "stream-of-commerce" concept adopted. The scope of Federal taxing power was also broadened expansively. In sanctioning the Social Security Act, the unemployment excise tax on employers was upheld as a legitimate use of

> the tax power, and the grants to the states were viewed as examples of Federal-state collaboration, not Federal coercion. The act's old-age and benefit provisions were deemed to be proper because "Congress may spend money in aid of general welfare." When combined, these decisions obviously amounted to last rites for judicial dual federalism.[46]

Although the Supreme Court was no longer viewed as a major obstacle for the expansion of grant-in-aid programs, external factors led to a reduction in federal assistance from 1939 to 1946 as Congress focused on defense-related issues during World War II. For example, federal grant-in-aid funding averaged $947 million from 1939 through 1946, less than half of the New Deal's peak. Following the War, the number of federal grant-in-aid programs began to increase at an accelerated pace, from 29 in 1945, to 71 in 1952, and to 132 in 1960.[47] Federal funding for grants-in-aid also accelerated, from $917 million in 1945, to $2.3 billion in 1952, and to $7 billion in 1960. A new development was increased funding for urban areas, such as grants for airport construction (1946), urban renewal (1949), and urban planning (1954). The most significant grant-in-aid program enacted during the 1950s was the $25 billion, 13-year Federal-Aid Highway Act of 1956, which authorized the construction of the then-41,000 mile National System of Interstate and Defense Highways, with a 1972 target completion date. For the next thirty-five years, federal surface transportation policy focused on the completion of the interstate system.[48]

THE GREAT SOCIETY AND THE RISE OF "COERCIVE FEDERALISM": 1960-1980

The 1960s was a turbulent decade, marked by both political and social upheaval of historic proportions. Three leading public figures were assassinated, President John F. Kennedy in 1963, civil rights leader the Reverend Martin Luther King, Jr. in 1968, and President Kennedy's brother, presidential candidate and Senator Robert Kennedy in 1968. The civil rights movement, led by the Reverend King, was often met with violent resistance, with bombings of black churches, murders of civil rights workers, and televised police beatings of civil rights demonstrators. One of the defining moments of the civil rights movement was the march on Washington D.C. in August 1963, where the Reverend King made his famous "I Have A Dream" speech. Congress responded to the social turmoil by adopting the Civil Rights

Act of 1964, which superseded state civil rights laws by prohibiting discrimination based on race, color, religion or national origin; the Voting Rights Act of 1965 which superseded state election laws by outlawing literacy tests, poll taxes and other means to discourage minority voting; and the Civil Rights Act of 1968 which superseded state civil rights laws by prohibiting discrimination in the sale, rental and financing of housing. Nonetheless, race riots took place in several urban areas in 1965 and in 1967.[49]

During the latter half of the decade, the civil rights movement was joined by what has been called the hippie movement, where young people rebelled against the conservative norms of the time and disassociated themselves from mainstream liberalism and materialism. This "counterculture" movement began in the United States and sparked a social revolution throughout much of the western world. It began as a reaction against the conservatism and social conformity of the 1950s, and the U.S. government's military intervention in Vietnam. These groups questioned authority and government, demanded more freedom and rights for women, gays, and minorities, and greater awareness of the need to protect the environment and address poverty.

The social movements and social unrest that swept across the nation during the 1960s had a strong impact on Congress. Reflecting the growing public demand for congressional action to address civil rights, poverty, and the environment, in 1961 the House approved, 217-212, a proposal by Speaker Sam Rayburn to enlarge the House Rules Committee from 12 to 15 members. Prior to the change, the House Rules Committee was divided, 6 to 6, along ideological lines. Because a majority vote is necessary for the issuance of a legislative rule, the House Rules Committee served as an institutional barrier to the passage of legislation that the committee's more conservative members believed infringed on states rights, including civil rights legislation.[50]

The enlargement of the House Rules Committee in 1961 signaled the weakening of the conservative coalition's influence within Congress and enabled the large Democratic majorities elected during the early 1960s in the House and Senate to adopt a succession of civil rights laws, highlighted by the previously mentioned Civil Rights Act of 1964. It also enabled Congress to increase dramatically, both in terms of numbers and funding, federal grants-in-aid to state and local governments designed to protect the environment and address poverty, both directly through public assistance and job training programs and indirectly through education, housing, nutrition, and health care programs.

These legislative efforts were both supported and encouraged by President Lyndon Baines Johnson. For example, during his commencement address at the University of Michigan on May 22, 1964, President Johnson announced that he would establish working groups to prepare a series of White House conferences and meetings to develop legislative proposals to revitalize urban America, address environmental problems, and improve educational opportunities "to begin to set our course toward the Great Society" which "demands an end to poverty and racial injustice, to which we are totally committed."[51] The term "The Great Society" came to symbolize legislative efforts during the 1960s to address poverty and racial injustice.

In concert with President Johnson's Great Society initiatives, Congress increased dramatically the number of federal grant-in-aid programs during the 1960s, from 132 in 1960 to 387 in 1968. In 1965 alone, 109 grant-in-aid programs were adopted, including Medicaid, which now has, by far, the largest budget of any grant-in-aid program. Funding for grants-in-aid also increased, from $7 billion in 1960 to $20 billion in 1969. Functionally, grant-in-aid funding for health care increased from $214 million in 1960 to $3.8 billion in 1970, for income security from $2.6 billion to $5.7 billion, for education, training, employment and social services from $525 million to $6.4 billion, for transportation from $3 billion to $4.6 billion, and for community and regional development from $109 million to $1.7 billion.[52]

For the most part, these legislative efforts were not opposed by state and local government officials and their affiliated public interest groups (e.g., National Governors Association, National League of Cities, U.S. Conference of Mayors, National Association of Counties, etc.), primarily because federal grant-in-aid programs are voluntary and, in many instances, provided funding for activities that had broad public support. However, the new grants had a number of innovative features that distinguished them from their predecessors. Previously, most federal grant-in-aid programs supplemented existing state efforts and, generally, did not intrude on state and local government prerogatives. Most of the grants created during the 1960s, on the other hand, were designed purposively by Congress to encourage state and local governments to move into new policy areas, or to expand efforts in areas identified by Congress as national priorities, especially in environmental protection and water treatment, education, public assistance, and urban renewal.[53]

There also was an increased emphasis on narrowly focused project, categorical grants to ensure that state and local governments were addressing national needs. In addition, most of the new grants had relatively low, or no, matching requirements, to encourage state and local government participation. There were also new incentive grants to encourage states to move into new policy areas, and a diversification of eligible grant recipients, including individuals, non-profit organizations, and specialized public institutions, such as universities. There was also a greater emphasis on grants to urban areas. For example, federal grant outlays targeted to metropolitan areas more than tripled during the 1960s, and grew to include about 70% of total federal grant funding, up from about 55% at the beginning of the decade. There was also a greater emphasis on mandated planning requirements.[54]

Although most of the grants adopted during the 1960s were narrowly focused project, categorical grants, the first two block grants were enacted during this time period. The Partnership for Public Health Act of 1966 created a block grant for comprehensive health care services (now the Preventive Health and Health Services Block Grant). It replaced nine formula categorical grants.[55] Two years later, Congress created the second block grant, the Law Enforcement Assistance Administration's Grants for Law Enforcement program (sometimes referred to as the "Crime Control" or "Safe Streets" block grant) in the Omnibus Crime Control and Safe Streets Act of 1968.[56] Unlike the health care services block grant, it was created *de novo*, and did not consolidate any existing categorical grants.[57]

The rapid expansion of grants-in-aid during the 1960s led to a growing concern that the intergovernmental grant-in-aid system had become dysfunctional and in need of reform. For example, ACIR argued that along with the expansion of the grant system came "a rising chorus of complaints from state and local government officials" concerning the inflexibility of fiscal and administrative requirements attached to the grants.[58] It suggested that state and local government officials were subjected to an information gap because they found it difficult to keep up with the host of new federal grant-in-aid programs and administrative requirements. It also cited the need for improved coordination among programs, noting that many state and local government officials were reporting administrative difficulties dealing with federal agencies and those agencies' regional offices:

> Between 1962 and 1965 four new systems of regional offices were established as a consequence of grants-in-aid legislation. Adding these bodies to the separate, already existing regional structures brought the total number of regional systems to 12. Regional boundaries and field office locations varied widely. Kentucky, to cite the most extreme case, had to deal with federal agencies in ten different cities. This confusion imposed burdens on the recipients of grants and also made the task of coordinating operations by federal agencies in pursuit of national objectives more difficult.[59]

During the 1970s, President Richard Nixon and his successor, President Gerald R. Ford, argued that the intergovernmental grant-in-aid system was dysfunctional and advocated the sorting out of governmental responsibilities, with the federal government taking the lead in some functional areas and states in others. They also advocated a shift from narrowly focused categorical grants, especially project categorical grants, toward block grants and revenue sharing. They argued that block grants and general revenue sharing provided state and local governments additional flexibility in project selection and promoted program efficiency by reducing administrative costs. They, and others, believed that state and local governments should be provided additional flexibility in project selection and relief from federal administrative requirements because

- greater reliance on state and local governments promotes a sense of state and local community responsibility and self-reliance;
- state and local government officials are closer to the people than federal administrators and, as a result, are better positioned to discern and adapt public programs to state and local needs and conditions;
- state and local governments encourage participation and civic responsibility by allowing more people to become involved in public questions;
- active state and local governments encourage experimentation and innovation in public policy design and implementation;
- active state and local governments reduce administrative work load on the federal government which creates program efficiencies; and
- active state and local governments reduce the political turmoil that sometimes results from single policies that govern the entire nation.[60]

Opponents of a shift from categorical grants to block grants and revenue sharing presented several arguments, including

- because funding comes from the federal treasury, Congress has both the right and the obligation to determine how that money is spent;
- many state and local governments lack the fiscal resources to provide levels of government services necessary to provide the poor and disadvantaged a minimum standard of living and equal access to governmental services, such as education and health care, that are essential to economic success. Therefore, Congress must act to ensure

uniform levels of essential governmental services throughout the nation;

- state and local governments that have the fiscal resources to provide levels of government services necessary to provide the poor and disadvantaged a minimum standard of living and equal access to governmental services essential to economic success are often unable to do so because they compete with other state and local governments for business and taxpaying residents. As a result, state and local governments tend to focus available resources on programs designed to attract business investment and taxpaying residents to their communities and states rather than on programs assisting the poor and disadvantaged. Therefore, Congress must act to ensure uniform levels of essential governmental services throughout the nation;
- Congress has both the right and the obligation to ensure through the carrot of grant-in-aid programs and the stick of federal requirements that certain national goals, such as civil rights, equal employment opportunities, protection for the environment, and care for the poor and aged, are met because it is difficult to achieve change when reform-minded citizens must deal with 50 state governments and more than 79,000 local governments; and
- there are some governmental services that have either costs or benefits that spill over onto other localities or states. Water and air pollution controls, for example, benefit not only the local community that pays for the air or water pollution controls, but all of the communities that are located downwind or downstream from that community. Because state and local taxpayers are generally reluctant to pay for programs whose benefits go to others, state and local governments often underfund programs with significant spillover effects. Therefore, Congress must act to ensure that these programs are funded at logical levels.[61]

Opponents also asserted that the arguments presented by advocates for a shift in emphasis to block grants and revenue sharing were actually a "smoke screen" masking their true intent which, allegedly, was to shift federal resources to their core constituencies. As mentioned previously, most grant-in-aid funding during the 1960s and 1970s was targeted to metropolitan areas, which, at that time, were considered Democratic Party strongholds. Many observers believed that shifting from project categorical grants to block grants or general revenue sharing would result in less money for metropolitan areas and more money for suburban and rural areas, areas that were more likely to be populated by Republicans than Democrats. This shift would occur because project categorical grants are awarded on a competitive basis by federal administrators while block grant and revenue sharing funding is allocated according to pre-determined formula, often with minimum funding guarantees for each state and with a portion of the funding determined by either population and/or per capita income. Because block grant and revenue sharing funding tends to be more geographically dispersed than project categorical grants, congressional debates over which grant mechanism was best had partisan overtones that often transcended discussions over which grant mechanism would improve grant performance.

Some federalism scholars have also suggested that Congress tends to prefer categorical grants over block grants and revenue sharing because Members take pride in the authorship of sponsored programs. They argue that categorical grants provide more opportunities for sponsorship, and more opportunities for receiving political credit for that sponsorship, than block grants or revenue sharing. In their view, constituents are more interested in a Members' ability to serve in a material way than in their competence in broad policymaking or in "the rightness of positions on issues of principle, form or structure."[62] As a result, they argue that Members are more likely to be recognized for sponsoring or supporting specific, narrowly focused categorical grants than by championing a more general block grant or revenue sharing approach. For example, they assert that Members are more likely to receive recognition and political credit from constituents for sponsoring and supporting legislation to prevent lead-based paint poisoning among children than for legislation covering the broad area of preventive health services.[63]

Presidents Nixon and Ford's efforts to gain congressional approval for a shift in emphasis from categorical grants to block grants and revenue sharing were only partially successful. For example, in his 1971 State of the Union speech, President Nixon announced a plan to consolidate 129 federal grant programs in six functional areas, 33 in education, 26 in transportation, 12 in urban community development, 17 in manpower training, 39 in rural community development, and 2 in law enforcement into what he called six "special revenue sharing" programs. Unlike the categorical grants they would replace, the proposed special revenue sharing programs had no state matching requirements, relatively few auditing or oversight requirements, and the funds were distributed automatically by formula without prior federal approval of plans for their use.[64]

The education, transportation, rural community development, and law enforcement proposals failed to gain congressional approval, primarily because they generated opposition from interest groups affiliated with the programs who worried that the programs' future funding would be compromised.[65] However, three block grants, the first signed by President Nixon and the remaining two signed by President Ford, were approved.

The Comprehensive Employment and Training Assistance Block Grant program, created by the Comprehensive Employment and Training Act of 1973, merged 17 existing manpower training categorical grant programs. The Community Development Block Grant program (CDBG), created by the Housing and Community Development Act of 1974, consolidated six existing community and economic development categorical grant programs.[66] Title XX social services, later renamed the Social Services Block Grant program, was created *de novo* and, therefore, did not consolidate any existing categorical grant programs. It was authorized by the 1974 amendments of the Social Security Act which was signed into law on January 4, 1975.[67] Also, in 1972, general revenue sharing was approved by Congress. General revenue sharing distributed funds to states from 1972 to 1981 and to localities from 1972 to 1986.

Nevertheless, Congress retained an emphasis on the use of categorical grants. On December 31, 1980, there were 534 categorical grant programs, 4 block grant programs and 1 general revenue sharing program. Of the categorical grant programs, 361 were project categorical grants, 42 were project, formula categorical grants, 111 were formula categorical grants, and 20 were open-ended reimbursement categorical grants.[68] Overall, categorical grants accounted for 79.3% of the $91.3 billion in federal grant-in-aid funding that year, block grants accounted for 11.3% and general revenue sharing 9.4%.[69]

Efforts to sort out governmental responsibilities were also met with resistance in Congress. For example, President Nixon's six special revenue sharing proposals would have provided state and local governments the leading role in decision-making in those six functional areas. Also, his proposed Family Assistance Plan would have replaced several public assistance categorical grant programs with a national public assistance system covering all low-income families with children. Although his Family Assistance Plan was not adopted, Congress did nationalize several adult-age public assistance grant-in-aid programs in 1972, including old-age assistance, aid to the blind, and aid to the permanently and totally disabled.[70]

Another Related Development: Federal Mandates

Another related, new development during the 1960s and 1970s was the imposition by Congress of numerous federal mandates on state and local government officials. The concept of mandates covers a broad range of policy actions with centralizing effects on the intergovernmental system, including statutory direct-order mandates, both total and partial statutory preemption of state and local government law, federal tax policies affecting state and local tax bases, and regulatory action taken by federal courts and agencies. Many federalism scholars also consider program specific and crosscutting grant-in-aid conditions mandates, even though the grants themselves are voluntary.[71]

Crosscutting requirements are, perhaps, the most widely recognized mandate. They are a condition of federal assistance that applies across-the-board to all, or most, federal grants to advance a national social or economic goal. Title VI of the Civil Rights Act of 1964 was the first post-World War II statute to use a crosscutting requirement. It specifies that

> No person in the United States shall, on the ground of race, color, or national origin, be excluded from participation in, be denied the benefits of, or be subjected to discrimination under any program receiving Federal financial assistance.[72]

In 1980, the U.S. Office of Management and Budget counted 59 crosscutting requirements intended to further national social or economic goals in a variety of functional areas, including education and the environment.[73]

Some of the statutory direct-order mandates adopted during this era included the Equal Employment Opportunity Act of 1972, which extended the prohibitions against discrimination in employment contained in the Civil Rights Act of 1964 to state and local government employment; the Fair Labor Standards Act Amendments of 1974, which extended the prohibitions against age discrimination in the Age Discrimination in Employment Act of 1967 to state and local government employment; and the Public Utilities Regulatory Policy Act of 1978, which established federal requirements concerning the pricing of electricity and natural gas.[74]

ACIR suggested that the expansion of federal intergovernmental regulatory activity during the 1960s and 1970s fundamentally changed the nature of intergovernmental relations in the United States:

> During the 1960s and 1970s, state and local governments for the first time were brought under extensive federal regulatory controls.... Over

> this period, national controls have been adopted affecting public functions and services ranging from automobile inspection, animal preservation and college athletics to waste treatment and waste disposal. In field after field the power to set standards and determine methods of compliance has shifted from the states and localities to Washington.[75]

The continued emphasis on categorical grants, the increased emphasis on provisions encouraging states to move in new policy directions, and, especially, the increased imposition of federal mandates on state and local governments during the 1960s and 1970s led some federalism scholars to label the 1960s and 1970s as the beginnings of a shift toward "coercive federalism."[76]

Cooperative features were still present, but congressional deference to state and local government prerogatives seen in previous eras was no longer in force. Instead of focusing primarily on the "carrot" of federal assistance to encourage state and local governments to pursue polices that aligned with national goals, Congress increasingly relied on the "stick" of federal mandates.

Congress Asserts Its Authority: The Devolution Revolution That Wasn't, 1980-2000

By the end of the 1970s, the social turmoil that marked the previous two decades had receded. Into the 1980s, America and the western world experienced a revival of conservative politics, the advancement of free market solutions to improve government efficiency and solve social problems, and a renewed emphasis on materialism and the possession of consumer goods.[77] Yet, at the same time, social change continued to affect American lifestyles, as women became fixtures in the workplace, the gay rights movement become more active, environmental concerns intensified, and rock concerts featuring the leading rock bands and performers of the era were televised to millions of viewers across the nation and the world to raise money for various social causes, such as famine relief, support for family farms, and AIDs prevention and treatment.

The seemingly contradictory societal trends of self-promotion and altruism that swept across American society during the 1980s and 1990s were reflected in responses to national public opinion polls concerning politics and government. These polls evidenced a growing public hostility toward government intrusion and government performance, especially the federal government's performance, despite growing support for specific programs and regulations that represented the polar opposite of these attitudes.[78] Perhaps reflecting these seemingly contradictory trends, during this era the public tended to elect a President of one political party and a Congress of another. Moreover, nationally, the two-party political system became more competitive as the once solid Democratic South turned increasing Republican. The Republican Party's resurgence was evidenced by its winning the presidency from 1981 to 1993, and its achieving majority status in the Senate from 1981 to 1987, and in both Houses of Congress from 1995 to 2001.

President Ronald Reagan's election in 1980, coupled with the Republican Party's resurgence, especially its winning majority party status in the Senate that year, signaled for some the potential for a "devolution revolution" in American federalism, where unfunded federal mandates would be rescinded, "burdensome" administrative grant-in-aid conditions removed, and the cooperative features of grant-in-aid programs enhanced. This belief was based on President Reagan's commitment to reducing the federal budget deficit. Because he was convinced that it was necessary to increase defense spending, President Reagan concluded that the only way to reduce the federal budget deficit was to increase revenue by encouraging economic growth through tax reduction and regulatory relief, and limiting the growth of federal domestic expenditures. As a former Governor, he trusted state and local governments' ability to provide essential government services. As a result, he advocated a sorting out of governmental responsibilities that would reduce the federal government's role in domestic affairs, increase the emphasis on block grants to provide state and local government officials greater flexibility in determining how the program's funds are spent, and impose fiscal restraint on all federal grant-in-aid programs.[79]

For example, on February 18, 1981, President Reagan addressed a joint session of Congress and proposed the consolidation of 84 existing categorical grants into 6 new block grants and requested significant funding reductions for a number of income maintenance categorical grants, including housing (rental) assistance, food stamps, Medicaid, and job training. Congress subsequently approved the Omnibus Budget Reconciliation Act of 1981, which consolidated 75 categorical grants and two earlier block grants into the following nine new block grants:

- Elementary and Secondary Education (37 categorical grants),
- Alcohol, Drug Abuse, and Mental Health Services (10 categorical grants),

- Maternal and Child Health Services (9 categorical grants),
- Preventive Health and Human Services Block Grant (merged 6 categorical grants with the Health Incentive Grants for Comprehensive Health Services Block Grant),
- Primary Care (2 categorical grants),
- Community Services (7 categorical grants),
- Social Services (one categorical grant and the Social Services for Low Income and Public Assistance Recipients Block Grant),
- Low-Income Home Energy Assistance (1 categorical grant), and
- revised the Community Development Block Grant program (adding an existing discretionary grant and 3 categorical grants).[80]

Overall, funding for the categorical grants bundled into these block grants was reduced 12%, about $1 billion, from their combined funding level the previous year.[81] President Reagan argued that the funding reductions would not result in the loss of services for recipients because the reductions would be offset by administrative efficiencies.

Some observers were convinced that the adoption of the Omnibus Budget Reconciliation Act of 1981 was proof of the coming devolution revolution. An unprecedented nine new block grants had been created during President Reagan's first year in office, the total number of grant-in-aid programs was reduced from 539 in 1981 to 441 in 1982, and total spending on grants-in-aid fell for the first time since World War II, from $94.8 billion in FY1981 to $88.2 billion in FY1982.[82] However, in retrospect, federalism scholars now consider the 1981 block grants as more "historical accidents than carefully conceived restructurings of categorical programs" because they were contained in a lengthy bill that was adopted under special parliamentary rules requiring a straight up or down vote without the possibility of amendment, the bill was designed to reduce the budget deficit not to reform federalism relationships, and the bill was not considered and approved by authorizing committees of jurisdiction.[83] Nonetheless, largely due to the Omnibus Budget and Reconciliation Act of 1981, in FY1984 there were 12 block grants in operation (compared to 392 categorical grants), accounting for about 15% of total grants-in-aid funding.[84]

During the remainder of his presidency, President Ronald Reagan submitted 26 block grant proposals to Congress, with only one, the Federal Transit Capital and Operating Assistance Block Grant, added in 1982. In addition, Congress approved the Job Training Partnership Act of 1982 which created a new block grant for job training to replace the block grant contained in the Comprehensive Employment and Training Act of 1973.[85]

Federalism scholars generally agree that President Reagan had unprecedented success in achieving congressional approval for block grants in 1981. However, they also note that most of President Reagan's subsequent block grant proposals failed to gain congressional approval, primarily because they were opposed by organizations who feared that, if enacted, the block grants would result in less funding for the affected programs. For example, in 1982, President Reagan proposed, but could not get congressional approval for, a $20 billion "swap" in which the federal government would return to states full responsibility for funding Aid to Families With Dependent Children (AFDC) (now Temporary Assistance for Needy Families) and food stamps in exchange for federal assumption of state contributions for Medicaid. As part of the deal, he also proposed a temporary $28 billion trust fund or "super revenue sharing program" to replace 43 other federal grant programs, including 19 social, health, and nutrition services programs, 11 transportation programs, 6 community development and facilities programs, 5 education and training programs, Low Income Home Energy Assistance, and general revenue sharing. The trust fund, and federal taxes supporting it, would begin phasing out after four years leaving states the option of replacing federal tax support with their own funds to continue the programs or allowing the programs to expire.[86]

Both the swap proposal and the proposed devolution of 43 federal grants failed to gain congressional approval, primarily because they were opposed by organizations and Members who feared that, if enacted, the proposals would result in less funding for the affected programs. For example, the National Governors Association supported the federal takeover of Medicaid, but objected to assuming the costs for AFDC and food stamps. The economy was weakening at that time and governors worried that they would not have the fiscal capacity necessary to support the programs without continued federal assistance.[87]

Evidence of a coming devolution revolution proved elusive as the upward trend in funding for grant-in-aid programs resumed in 1983, although at a somewhat lower rate of increase than during the previous two decades. As shown in **Table 2**, federal grant-in-aid funding increased from $91 billion in FY1980 to $135 billion in FY1990 and $285.8 billion in FY2000. Medicaid accounted for much of that revenue growth, increasing from $13.9 billion in FY1980 to $41.1 billion in FY1990 and $117.9 billion in FY2000.[88]

Functionally, as shown in **Table 2**, federal grant-in-aid funding for health care increased from $15.7 billion in FY1980 to $124.8 billion in FY2000. Also, grant-in-aid funding increased for income security from $18.4 billion in FY1980 to $68.6 billion in FY2000; for education, training, employment and social services from $21.8 billion to $36.6 billion; for transportation from $13 billion to $32.2 billion; and for community and regional development from $6.4 billion to $8.6 billion.

The number of grant-in-aid programs did fall at the beginning of this era, from 539 in 1980 to an era low of 405 in 1984, but then resumed their upward trend. As indicated in **Table 4**, there were 539 grant-in-aid programs in 1980, 557 in 1991, and 664 in 1998. Moreover, the number of intergovernmental mandates continued to increase throughout the era. ACIR, for example, identified 36 significant federal mandates affecting state and local governments in 1980. In 1990, it identified 63.[89] ACIR concluded that "despite efforts to constrain the growth of intergovernmental regulation, the 1980s remained an era of regulatory expansion rather then contraction."[90] It offered the following explanation for the increased number of federal mandates during the 1980s:

> The causes of this continued regulatory growth are complex and varied. Many regulations address important and well documented problems from pollution to health care to civil rights. The goals associated with these programs are popular not only with the general public but with state and local government officials as well. But, whereas the Congress in the past might have responded to emerging needs with a new federal aid program, the scarcity of federal funds during a decade of historic deficits has made the alternative of federal mandates look increasingly attractive to federal policymakers.[91]

Some observers believed that the anticipated devolution revolution might be realized following the 1994 congressional elections which resulted in the Republican Party gaining majority status in both the House and Senate. As evidence of the potential for a devolution revolution they pointed to the Unfunded Mandate Reform Act of 1995 (UMRA). Its intent was to limit the federal government's ability to impose costs on state and local governments or on the private sector through unfunded mandates. Providing relief from unfunded mandates was one of the stated goals of the Republican Party's 1994 Contract With America.[92]

Under UMRA, congressional committees have the initial responsibility to identify certain federal mandates in measures under consideration. If the measure contains a federal mandate, the authorizing committee must provide the measure to the Congressional Budget Office (CBO). It reports back to the committee an estimate of the mandate's costs. The office must prepare full quantitative estimates for each reported measure with mandate costs over pre-determined thresholds in any of the first five fiscal years the legislation would be in effect. CBO's cost estimates include the direct costs of the federal mandates contained in the measure, or in any necessary implementing regulations; and the amount of new or existing federal funding the legislation authorizes to pay these costs. The thresholds triggering a full CBO cost estimate are adjusted annually for inflation. They were originally $50 million for intergovernmental mandates and $100 million for private sector mandates. The thresholds in 2012 are $73 million for intergovernmental mandates and $146 million for private sector mandates. CBO must prepare brief statements of cost estimates for those mandates that have estimated costs below these thresholds.[93]

Members can raise a point of order if the measure containing the mandate lacks a CBO cost estimate, either because the Committee failed to publish the CBO's cost estimate in its report or in the *Congressional Record*, or CBO determined that no reasonable estimate of the mandate's cost was feasible. Members can also raise a point of order if the measure has an intergovernmental cost estimate that exceeds the annually adjusted cost threshold ($71 million in 2011) in any of the first five fiscal years the mandate would be in effect.

UMRA's impact on unfunded mandates has been relatively limited. For example, from 1996 to February 2012, 47 points of order were raised in the House and 3 in the Senate. One point of order, concerning a 1996 minimum wage bill, was sustained in the House and two points of order, concerning amendments relating to an increase in the minimum wage in 2005, were sustained in the Senate.[94] In addition, UMRA covers only certain types of unfunded federal mandates. As one federalism scholar recently argued:

> UMRA primarily covers only statutory direct orders, excluding most grant conditions and preemptions whose fiscal effects fall below the threshold. Statutory direct orders dealing with constitutional rights, prohibition of discrimination, national security, and Social Security are among those excluded from coverage. Moreover, analytic and procedure requirements do not apply to appropriations bills, floor amendments or conference reports – those tools of "unorthodox lawmaking" that have become increasingly prevalent in the Congress.[95]

Moreover, another federalism scholar noted that the overall record of the 104th Congress, expected by some to decentralize and devolve federalism relationships, was more status quo than devolutionary:

> Shifting back to the overall record of the 104th Congress, it is appropriate here to note the various proposed devolutionary bills that were defeated. Chief among these was the proposed Medicaid block grant with a $163 billion cut in funding over five years. Both a public housing blocking proposal and the big regulatory reform measure that would have seriously limited the Federal government's power to issue rules affecting health, safety, and the environment were scuttled. Extension of the Clean Water Act, enactment of a consolidation of eighty-odd manpower training programs, and passage of a revised Endangered Species Act, which eliminated the Federal authority to restrict threatening activities, were all successfully resisted. A rollback of affirmative action, a conservative shift in the Superfund's program and rules, and the proposed Product Liability Legal Reform Act of 1996 were also scuttled. Of the nine here, two died because of Senate rejection; three, because of a presidential veto or the threat of one; two others failed because neither chamber dared take either one up; and the last two died because of a deadlocked Conference Committee and a lack of time to consider a Conference Report.[96]

The devolution revolution never fully materialized during this era, despite growing public hostility toward the federal government. The emphasis on categorical grants and the issuance of federal mandates continued. Yet, some decentralization of decision-making authority did take place during the era. For example, in 1980, there were four block grants in operation. In 2000, there were 24 block grants, including the Surface Transportation Program (1991) and the Temporary Assistance for Needy Families (TANF) program (1996). Funded at $16.7 billion annually, TANF rivaled the Surface Transportation Program during this era for the largest budget of all the block grants. In addition, Congress authorized state waivers for Medicaid starting in 1981, and for child welfare assistance programs starting in 1994.[97]

The seemingly contradictory trends of centralization and decentralization that took place in federal grant-in-aid programs during the 1980s and 1990s perhaps reflected the contradictory societal trends that swept across America at the time. As mentioned previously, national public opinion polls indicated that the public was increasingly dissatisfied with the performance of government, especially the federal government's performance, and expressed a growing hostility toward government (and Congress) as a whole. It could be argued that these views suggest that the public wanted Congress to devolve federal grant-in-aid programs to state and local governments or, at least, provide them greater flexibility in determining how grant-in-aid funding should be spent. Yet, at the same time, the public also expressed relatively strong support for individual federal government programs (and individual members of Congress).[98] It could be argued that these views suggest that the public wanted Congress to maintain federal government control over these programs, and expressed approval of their individual Members for doing so.

Another possible explanation for the continued focus on categorical grants and the imposition of federal mandates during this era is that federalism issues tend to be a second order priority for many federal policymakers. For example, it could be argued that President Ronald Reagan's commitment to strengthening federalism through program decentralization and devolution was unrivaled in the modern era. Yet, in an analysis of the Reagan Administration's federalism policies, a leading federalism scholar concluded that "devolutionary policies consistent with the president's definition of federalism reform ... consistently lost out in the Reagan Administration when they ... conflicted with the sometimes competing goals of reducing the federal deficit, deregulating the private sector, and advancing the conservative social agenda."[99] For example, this scholar noted that President Reagan opposed the expansion of General Revenue Sharing, advocated the elimination of the deductibility of state and local taxes, supported the preemption of state laws regulating double-trailer trucks and establishing minimum drinking ages, overrode state objections to increased off-shore oil drilling and increased use of nuclear power, and supported efforts to require states to establish workfare programs for public assistance recipients and suing localities which sought to retain aggressive affirmative action hiring policies.[100]

GRANTS-IN-AID IN THE 21ST CENTURY

Every nation has experienced defining moments that affect the collective social consciousness of nearly every person in that nation. These events tend to occur about once a generation, and often have a significant and lasting affect on political life. In the United States, the bombing of Pearl Harbor on December 7, 1941—"a date which will live in infamy"—the assassination of President John F. Kennedy on November 22, 1963, and the terrorist attacks on the World Trade Center in New York City and the Pentagon in Washington, DC, on September 11, 2001, were such moments. Nearly every adult in the nation alive at the time of these events, and many children as well, can recall where they were and what they were doing when they heard the news of these events.

It may be too soon to fully recognize the impact of 9/11 on American politics. However, for grants-in-aid, and American federalism, the short-term impact was clear: the centralization of governmental authority and an expansion of grants-in-aid programs and funding in homeland security and related emergency management areas.

Prior to September 11, 2001, the federal government had three categorical grants-in-aid programs pertinent to homeland security: the State Domestic Preparedness program administered by the Department of Justice, the Emergency Management Performance Grant program administered by the Federal Emergency Management Agency, and the Metropolitan Medical Response System administered by the Department of Health and Human Services. In FY2010, the Department of Homeland Security had 22 federal grant programs providing state and local governments assistance for training, exercises, the purchase of equipment, and other support for terrorism and disaster preparedness and response activities, including 19 categorical grant programs and the following three block grant programs: State Homeland Security Grants, formerly called the State Domestic Preparedness Program, (created in 2003), Urban Area Security Initiative Grants (created in 2003), and the Regional Catastrophic Preparedness Grant (created in 2008).[101] Moreover, national guidelines for emergency preparedness, governing such areas as equipment, training, and exercises and planning assisted with federal funds were issued by the Department of Homeland Security identifying target capabilities for 36 areas of emergency planning and response by state and local governments. Also, national mass transit and driver's license security standards were imposed. The National Governors Association and the National Conference of State Legislatures estimated in 2006 that the new driver's license security standards adopted in 2005 would cost states about $11 billion over five years to implement.[102]

Some observers thought that both the number of grants-in-aid and funding for grants-in-aid might fall during the George W. Bush's presidency, given the budgetary pressures created by President Bush's war on terror and his commitment to reducing the federal budget deficit, and the Republican Party's winning majority status in the House of Representatives from 2001 to 2007 and in the Senate for portions of 2001 and 2002, and from 2003 to 2007. Yet, funding for federal grant-in-aid programs increased during his presidency, from $285.8 billion in FY2000 to $461.3 billion in FY2008. Since then, federal grant-in-aid funding has accelerated and is now expected to reach

$612.4 billion in FY2012. Medicaid has accounted for much of the expenditure growth, increasing from $117.9 billion in FY2000 to $201.4 billion in FY2008, and an estimated $255.3 billion in FY2012, but funding has increased in other areas as well.[103] As shown in **Table 2**, grant-in-aid funding for health care is expected to increase from $124.8 billion in FY2000 to an estimated $275.2 billion in FY2012. Grant-in-aid funding for income security is expected to increase from $68.6 billion in FY2000 to an estimated $106.2 billion in FY2012; for education, training, employment, and social services, from $36.6 billion to $114.8 billion; for transportation, from $32.2 billion to $66.7 billion; and for community and regional development, from $8.6 billion to $17.7 billion.

The number of grant-in-aid programs also increased during the first decade of the 2000s, from 664 in 1998 to 953 in 2009. In addition, the emphasis on categorical grants was retained, as 928 of the 953 grants-in-aid in 2009 were categorical grants, and 25 were block grants.[104]

As shown in **Table 4**, these trends have continued under the Obama Administration. The number of grant-in-aid programs increased to 996 in 2012, and the emphasis on categorical grants has continued, as 968 of the 996 grants-in-aid in 2012 are categorical grants, and 28 are block grants.

Also, despite UMRA, unfunded federal mandates continued to be issued in several functional areas. For example, during the 109th Congress legislation was adopted that required states to collect data on sex offenders and to prepare a statewide sex offender registry database; imposed federal standards requiring state and local governments using federal foster care funding to visit foster care children monthly; and required states to hold special elections when continuity of government is jeopardized by a national emergency, necessitating some states to amend their state constitutions. Congress also preempted state and local government authority by prohibiting the use of federal grant funds for projects where eminent domain is used to support private uses; prohibited state and local government lawsuits against manufacturers or sellers of firearms; and regulating the citing of certain transmission lines and the citing and operation of onshore liquefied natural gas facilities, energy efficiency and safety of nuclear facilities, and the reliability of electric services.[105] In addition, CBO reported that 258 public laws were enacted in 2010, and 29 of those laws contained at least one intergovernmental mandate as defined in the Unfunded Mandates Reform Act. CBO found that these 29 laws contained a total of 86 intergovernmental mandates, which was "significantly higher than in previous years."[106]

Grant conditions, historically the predominant means used to impose federal control over state and local government actions, continued to be used to promote national goals. For example, many observers consider the adoption of the No Child Left Behind Act of 2001, signed into law on January 8, 2002, to be President George W. Bush's signature federalism achievement. Although the act allows states to define the standards used for testing, it imposed federal testing, teaching, and accountability standards on states and school districts that, overall, significantly increased federal influence on public elementary and secondary education throughout the nation.[107] In addition, the Help America Vote Act of 2002 instituted "sweeping new federal standards, along with new funding, that regulated significant features of state and local election processes."[108]

President Obama has not issued a formal federalism plan and has not advocated a major shift in funding priorities either within functional categories or from categorical grants to block grants. However, his Administration, and Congress, have continued to use federal grants-in-aid as a means to achieve national goals. For example, in its FY2011 budget request to Congress the Obama Administration argued that it was in the national interest to increase federal assistance to state and local governments at that time because the additional funding would enable state and local governments to avoid "taking steps that would have otherwise harmed economic growth and cost jobs" as they coped with large budget shortfalls caused, in large part, by a decline in revenue related to the economic downturn.[109] The Obama Administration argued that a Council of Economic Advisors' analysis had found a positive relationship between the additional funding provided under ARRA and employment "in such areas as public safety, education, health care, and other sectors where state governments provide a large amount of financial support."[110] As mentioned previously, ARRA is expected to provide about $300 billion for federal grant-in-aid programs for state and local governments. ARRA provides additional funding for a wide range of federal grant-in-aid programs, such as Medicaid ($93 billion, primarily for a temporary increase in the Federal Medical Assistance Percentages reimbursement rate), a new, State Fiscal Stabilization Fund ($53.6 billion), Build America Bonds ($30 billion), Highways and Bridges ($27.5 billion), Title 1-A, elementary and secondary education for the disadvantaged, ($13 billion), Individuals with Disabilities Education Act ($12.2 billion), Public Transit ($8.4 billion), Intercity Passenger Rail Capital, Congestion, and Corridor Development grants ($8 billion), Temporary Assistance for Needy Families ($5 billion), and Weatherization Assistance Grants ($5 billion).[111]

In addition, the Obama Administration argued in its FY2013 budget request to Congress that its funding recommendations for federal aid to state and local governments were guided by its interest in "investing in areas that promote growth, job creation, and constructing an economy that is built to last."[112] Also, because "economic conditions at the state level are slowly improving" the Obama Administration recommended that federal aid to state and local governments continue to increase over the next several fiscal years, but at lower rates of growth than experienced in recent fiscal years.[113]

CONGRESSIONAL ISSUES

As the data in **Table 2**, **Table 3**, and **Table 4** attest, federal grant-in-aid expenditures, in both nominal and constant dollars, and the number of intergovernmental grants have continued to increase since the mid-1980s. Given its increased size and cost, providing effective congressional oversight of the intergovernmental grant-in-aid system is a daunting task. Given the decentralized nature of the congressional committee system, Congress is well-positioned to provide effective oversight of individual federal grant-in-aid programs. However, it could be argued that the decentralized nature of the congressional committee system is not optimally conducive to providing effective oversight of the interactive effects of multiple federal grant-in-aid programs, or of the potential interactive effects of federal grant-in-aid spending programs and federal tax policy.

In the past, the independent, bipartisan ACIR, which operated from 1959 to 1996, provided Congress and others a series of authoritative reports on the status and operation of intergovernmental grants-in-aid programs, both as individual programs and as a collective system. GAO has published several reports over the years on federal grant-in-aid programs that have helped to fill the informational and analytic void left by ACIR's demise.[114] However, it could be argued that Congress may wish to examine whether a reconstituted ACIR, perhaps one that focuses on the structure and operation of the intergovernmental system as a whole, might prove useful as an additional source of information and analysis as it conducts oversight of the intergovernmental federal grant-in-aid system. For example, such an organization could provide an accepted methodology for counting grants-in-aid programs, and provide Congress periodic assessments of the intergovernmental grant-in-aid system's performance.

Another potential congressional issue of interest is that neither the House nor the Senate currently has in place a committee or subcommittee that is dedicated solely to the oversight of intergovernmental issues. In the past, both the House and the Senate have had in place a subcommittee dedicated to the oversight of intergovernmental issues, typically focusing on the structure and operation of federal grant-in-aid programs and federal mandates. Congress may wish to consider whether the recent growth in the number of intergovernmental grant-in-aid programs and the increased funding for federal grants warrants the formation of either a committee or a subcommittee whose primary focus is the examination of intergovernmental issues.

CONCLUSION

It could be argued that the recent upward trend in federal grant-in-aid funding is about to end because ARRA's funding is expiring and there is a general consensus that anticipated growth in federal discretionary spending, which includes federal grant-in-aid funding, may be targeted for reductions as part of an effort to address the federal debt. However, President Obama's recommended use of grant-in-aid programs to create jobs and promote national economic growth, and Congress's historical tendency to approve that strategy, suggests that the upward trend in grant funding and grant numbers that has been experienced over the past several decades may continue, although at a slower pace. President Obama's FY2013 budget, for example, anticipates that federal outlays for grant-in-aid programs will continue to increase from an estimated $612.4 billion in FY2012 to $632.7 billion in FY2013 and $662.1 billion in FY2014.[115]

In retrospect, with the exception of the early 1980s, grant funding, the number of grants, and the issuance of federal mandates, have increased under both Democratic and Republican Congresses and Presidents. Historically, there have been notable differences between the two parties' approaches toward federalism. Although both parties have generally opposed unfunded federal mandates, the Republican Party has done so more aggressively, as evidenced by its 1994 Contract With America and sponsorship of UMRA. The Republican Party has also advocated the devolution of certain grant-in-aid programs to state and local governments while the Democratic Party has generally opposed devolution. The Republican Party has also been more aggressive in its support of the decentralization of grants-in-aid decision-making to state and local governments through the consolidation of categorical grants into block grants, support for revenue sharing, and advocacy of administrative relief from various grant conditions. But, overall, the historical record suggests that for Members of both political parities, regardless of their personal ideological preferences, federalism principles often lose out when in conflict with other policy goals, such as reducing the federal budget deficit, promoting social values or environmental protection, and guaranteeing equal treatment and opportunity for the disadvantaged. As long at this continues to be the case, and the public continues to express support for specific government programs, even though they oppose "big" government as a whole, there is little evidence to suggest that the general historical trends of increasing numbers of grant-in-aid programs, increasing funding for grant-in-aid programs, an emphasis on categorical grants, and continued enactment of federal mandates, both funded and unfunded, is likely to change.

End Notes

[1] U.S. Congressional Budget Office, *The Budget and Economic Outlook: Fiscal Years 2010 to 2020* (Washington, DC: GPO, January 2010), p. 95, http://www.cbo.gov/sites/default/files/cbofiles/ftpdocs/108xx/doc10871/01-26-outlook.pdf. CBO's original cost estimate for ARRA from FY2009 through FY2019 was $787 billion.

[2] Ibid., pp. 95-98; and U.S. Government Accountability Office, *RECOVERY ACT: Status of States' and Localities' Use of Funds and Efforts to Ensure Accountability*, GAO-10-231, December 2009, p. 1, http://www.gao.gov/new.items/ d10231.pdf. GAO estimates that ARRA will provide state and local governments about $273 billion through 2016. See U.S. Government Accountability Office, "Following the Money: GAO's Oversight of the Recovery Act," Washington, DC, http://www.gao.gov/recovery/.

[3] U.S. Advisory Commission on Intergovernmental Relations (ACIR), *Categorical Grants: Their Role and Design*, A52 (Washington, DC: GPO, 1978), p. 61.

[4] Ibid.

[5] Samuel H. Beer, "The Modernization of American Federalism," in *Toward '76 – The Federal Polity*, special issue of *Publius: The Journal of Federalism*, vol. 3, no 2 (Fall 1973), pp. 49-95; and David B. Walker, *The Rebirth of Federalism*, 2nd Edition (NY: Chatham House Publishers, 2000), pp. 19-35.

[6] U.S. Advisory Commission on Intergovernmental Relations, *Categorical Grants: Their Role and Design*, A-52 (Washington, DC: GPO, 1978), pp. 5, 6.

[7] For further information and analysis concerning general revenue sharing, see CRS Report RL31936, *General Revenue Sharing: Background and Analysis*, by Steven Maguire.

[8] U.S. Congressional Budget Office, *The Budget and Economic Outlook: Fiscal Years 2010 to 2020* (Washington, DC: GPO, January 2010), p. 95, http://www.cbo.gov/sites/default/files/cbofiles/ftpdocs/108xx/doc10871/01-26-outlook.pdf.

[9] Includes the School Breakfast Program, the National School Lunch Program, and other nutrition programs.

[10] U.S. Office of Management and Budget, *Budget of the United States Government, Fiscal Year 2010: Historical Tables* (Washington, DC: GPO, 2009), pp. 239, 240, http://www.gpoaccess.gov/usbudget/fy10/pdf/hist.pdf. Note: The percentages were derived by dividing the difference between expenditures for the ninth year of the decade and the first year of the decade by expenditures for the first year of the decade.

[11] John Kincaid, "Developments in Federal-State Relations, 1992-93," *The Book of the States, 1994-95* (Lexington, KY: The Council of State Governments, 1994), pp. 576-586; and John Kincaid, "Trends in Federalism, Continuity, Change and Polarization," *The Book of the States, 2004* (Lexington, KY: The Council of State Governments, 2004), pp. 21-27.

[12] U.S. General Services Administration, *The Catalog of Federal Domestic Assistance* (Washington, DC: GPO, 2009), p. I.

[13] ACIR, *A Catalog of Federal Grant-In-Aid Programs to State and Local Governments: Grants Funded FY 1975*, A-52a (Washington, DC: GPO, 1977); ACIR, *A Catalog of Federal Grant-In-Aid Programs to State and Local Governments: Grants Funded FY 1978*, A-72 (Washington, DC: GPO, 1979); ACIR, *A Catalog of Federal Grant-InAid Programs to State and Local Governments: Grants Funded FY 1981*, M-133CAT (Washington, DC: GPO, 1982); ACIR, *A Catalog of Federal Grant-In-Aid Programs to State and Local Governments: Grants Funded FY 1984*, M-139 (Washington, DC: GPO, 1984); ACIR, *A Catalog of Federal Grant-In-Aid Programs to State and Local Governments: Grants Funded FY 1987*, M-153 (Washington, DC: GPO, 1987); ACIR, *A Catalog of Federal Grant-In-Aid Programs to State and Local Governments: Grants Funded FY 1989*, M-167 (Washington, DC: GPO, 1989); ACIR, *Characteristics of Federal Grant-In-Aid Programs to State and Local Governments: Grants Funded FY 1991*, M-182 (Washington, DC: GPO, 1992); ACIR, *Characteristics of Federal Grant-In-Aid Programs to State and Local Governments: Grants Funded FY 1993*, M-188 (Washington, DC: GPO, 1994); and ACIR, *Characteristics of Federal Grant-In-Aid Programs to State and Local Governments: Grants Funded FY 1995*, M-195 (Washington, DC: GPO, 1995).

[14] U.S. Office of Management and Budget (OMB), "The Number of Federal Grant Programs to State and Local Governments: 1980-2003," Washington, DC: OMB, February 18, 2004. Note: the Government Accountability Office provided a count for FY 1990, see U.S. General Accounting Office, *Federal Aid: Programs Available to State and Local Governments*, HRD 91-93FS, May 1991, http://archive.gao.gov/d20t9/143936.pdf.

[15] U.S. Office of Management and Budget (OMB), "The Number of Federal Grant Programs to State and Local Governments: 1980-2003," Washington, DC: OMB, February 18, 2004.

[16] ACIR excluded grants directly to profit-making institutions, individuals, and nonprofit institutions (unless such payments result in cash or in-kind services or products that are passed on to state or local governments); payments for research and development not directly related to the provision of services to the general public; payments for services rendered; grants to cover administrative expenses for regional bodies; loans and loan guarantees; and shared revenues. See, ACIR, *Characteristics of Federal Grant-In-Aid Programs to State and Local Governments: Grants Funded FY 1995* (Washington, DC: GPO, 1995), pp. 26-28, http://www.library.unt.edu/gpo/acir/Reports/information/M-195.pdf.

[17] U.S. Office of Management and Budget (OMB), "The Number of Federal Grant Programs to State and Local Governments: 1980-2003," Washington, DC: OMB, February 18, 2004, p. 7.

[18] The number of federal grants-in-aid programs was determined by first examining all entries in the CFDA's print version and then cross-checking the findings against a search using the

frequently updated CFDA's on-line search engine. Because the CFDA's on-line search engine includes subparts of programs, the following search terms were used to minimize this problem: assistance types (formula grants, project grants, direct payments for specified uses, and direct payments for unrestricted uses) by beneficiary eligibility (state governments, local governments, U.S. territories, and/or federally recognized tribal governments).

[19] Harry N. Scheiber, *The Condition of American Federalism: An Historian's View*, a study submitted by the Subcommittee on Intergovernmental Relations to the Committee on Government Operations, U.S. Senate, 89th Cong., 2nd sess., October 15, 1966; and Harry N. Scheiber, "Federalism and Legal Process: Historical and Contemporary Analyses of the American System," *Law & Civil Society Review*, vol. 14, no. 3 (Spring 1980), pp. 669-683. Note: There were aspect of cooperative federalism during this time period as well. For example, state officials administered federal elections, state governments housed some federal prisoners, and state courts tried some federal court cases, see Daniel J. Elazar, *The American Partnership: Federal-State Cooperation in the Nineteenth Century United States* (Chicago, IL: University of Chicago Press, 1962).

[20] *Journals of the Continental Congress, 1774-1789*, Volume XXVIII, May 20, 1785, p. 378, http://lcweb2.loc.gov/cgibin/query/r?ammem/hlaw:@field(DOCID+@lit(jc0281). Note: Proceeds from the sale of the four lots set aside for the United States were intended to fund promised military officer pensions and claims for back pay for military service during the Revolutionary War. Soldiers were also eligible for grants of land as compensation for these purposes, see pp. 379-380.

[21] Ibid., p. 378.

[22] Note: The Northwest Ordinance of 1787 ended state claims to the Ohio Country, established a territorial government for the region, included civil rights provisions that served as a precursor for the Bill of Rights, mandated that new states could be formed out of the territory once an area in the region reached a population of 60,000, and prohibited slavery in the region.

[23] Matthias Nordberg Orfield, "Federal Land Grants to the States With Special Reference to Minnesota," *Bulletin of the University of Minnesota*, Minneapolis, MN, March 1915, p. 42.

[24] For example, in *McCulloch v. Maryland*, 17 U.S. (4 Wheat.) 316 (1819), the Marshall Court established the doctrine of implied national powers, ruling that while federal powers were limited to those enumerated in the Constitution, the necessary and proper clause found in Article 1, Section 8, enlarged, rather than narrowed, congressional authority to act: "Let the end be legitimate, let it be within the scope of the Constitution, and all means which are appropriate, which are plainly adapted to that end, which are not prohibited, but consist with the letter and spirit of the Constitution, are constitutional." For further analysis, see CRS Report RL30315, *Federalism, State Sovereignty, and the Constitution: Basis and Limits of Congressional Power*, by Kenneth R. Thomas.

[25] Constitution of the United States, text available on the National Archives website: http://www.archives.gov/exhibits/ charters/bill_ofjights_transcript.html.

[26] Thomas Aquinas Burke, "Ohio Lands – A Short History," 8th ed. (Columbus, OH: State Auditor's Office, September 1996), http://freepages.history.rootsweb.ancestry.com/ ~maggie/ohio-lands/ohl5.html# WROTLNDS.

[27] Benjamin Horace Hibbard, *A History of the Public Land Policies* (New York: The Macmillan Company, 1924), pp. 228-233. Note: Maine and West Virginia were not eligible for the guarantee because they were formed out of other states and Texas was ineligible because it was considered a sovereign nation when admitted to the Union. Also, five states,

Wisconsin, Alabama, Iowa, Nevada and Oregon, subsequently were permitted to use their proceeds from federal land sales solely for public education.

[28] Matthias Nordberg Orfield, *Federal Land Grants to the States With Special Reference to Minnesota* (Minneapolis, MN: Bulletin of the University of Minnesota, 1915), pp. 77- 111, 115-118; Morton Grodzins, *The American System* (Chicago: Rand McNally, 1966), p. 35; Gary M. Anderson and Dolores T. Martin, "The Public Domain and Nineteenth Century Transfer Policy," *Cato Journal*, vol. 6, no. 3 (Winter 1987): 908-910; John Bell Rae, "Federal Land Grants in Aid of Canals," *The Journal of Economic History*, vol. 4, no. 2 (November 1944): 167, 168; and U.S. Department of Transportation, Federal Highway Administration, *America's Highways, 1776/1976* (Washington, DC: GPO, 1976), 24. Note: 26 states received federal land grants during the 1800s.

[29] President Franklin Pierce, "Message from the President of the United States returning a bill entitled "An act making a grant of public lands to the several States for the benefit of indigent insane persons" with a statement of the objections which have required him to withhold from it his approval to the United States Senate," 33rd Cong., 1st sess., Exec. Doc. 56, May 3, 1854.

[30] Henry Franklin Graff, editor, *The Presidents: A Reference History* (New York: Charles Scribner's Sons, 2002), pp. 118, 119; and Joseph A. Pechman, *Federal Tax Policy* (Washington, DC: The Brookings Institution, 1971), p. 290.

[31] Harry N. Scheiber, "State Law and 'Industrial Policy' in American Development, 1790-1987," *California Law Review*, vol. 75, no. 1 (January 1987), p. 419.

[32] David B. Walker, *The Rebirth of Federalism*, 2nd ed. (New York: Chatham House Publishers, 2000), p. 74.

[33] Robert A. Dahl, *Pluralist Democracy in the United States: Conflict and Consent* (Chicago: Rand McNally, 1967), pp. 318-319.

[34] 15 Stat. 2 ff; 15 Stat. 14 ff; and 15 Stat. 41.

[35] David B. Walker, *The Rebirth of Federalism*, 2nd ed. (New York: Chatham House Publishers, 2000), p. 75. The most famous civil rights case during this time period was *Plessy v. Ferguson* 163 U.S. 537 (1896) which upheld the constitutionality of state-imposed racial segregation.

[36] Cynthia Cates Colella, "The United States Supreme Court and Intergovernmental Relations," in *American Intergovernmental Relations Today: Perspectives and Controversies*, ed. Robert Jay Dilger (Englewood Cliffs, NJ: Prentice-Hall, Inc., 1986), p. 43. Note: In *Interstate Commerce Commission v. Brimson* 154 U.S. 447 (1894), the Court curtailed the ICC's hearing capacity and in *Interstate Commerce Commission v. Cincinnati, New Orleans and Texas Pacific Railway Company,* 167 U.S. 479 (1897) it ruled against the ICC's authority to fix rates.

[37] Morton Grodzins, *The American System* (Chicago: Rand McNally, 1966), pp. 35, 37.

[38] Ibid., p. 34.

[39] ACIR, *Categorical Grants: Their Role and Design*, A-52 (Washington, DC: GPO, 1978), pp. 15, 16.

[40] Cynthia Cates Colella, "The United States Supreme Court and Intergovernmental Relations," in *American Intergovernmental Relations Today: Perspectives and Controversies*, ed. Robert Jay Dilger (Englewood Cliffs, NJ: Prentice-Hall, Inc., 1986), p. 47.

[41] Valdimer Orlando Key, "A Theory of Critical Elections," *The Journal of Politics*, vol. 17, no. 1 (February 1955), pp. 3-18; Walter Dean Burnham, *Critical Elections and the Mainsprings of American Politics* (New York: W.W. Norton & Company, 1970); and David R. Mayhew,

Electoral Realignments: A Critique of an American Genre (New Haven: Yale University Press, 2002).

[42] ACIR, *Categorical Grants: Their Role and Design*, A-52 (Washington, DC: GPO, 1978), pp. 18, 19.

[43] Ibid., p. 18.

[44] Ibid., p. 20.

[45] David B. Walker, *The Rebirth of Federalism*, 2nd ed. (New York: Chatham House Publishers, 2000), p. 91. Note: President Roosevelt proposed that he be given the authority to appoint another judge for each one who had served ten years or more and had not retired within six months of their 70th birthday. A maximum of 50 such appointments were to be permitted, and the Supreme Court's size was to be increased to 15.

[46] Ibid., p. 92.

[47] ACIR, *Categorical Grants: Their Role and Design*, A-52 (Washington, DC: GPO, 1978), pp. 22-24.

[48] For further analysis, see CRS Report R40431, *Federalism Issues in Surface Transportation Policy: Past and Present*, by Robert Jay Dilger; and CRS Report R40053, *Surface Transportation Program Reauthorization Issues for the 111th Congress*, coordinated by John W. Fischer.

[49] David B. Walker, *The Rebirth of Federalism: Slouching Toward Washington* (Chatham, NJ: Chatham House Publishers, Inc., 1995), p. 125; and Theodore H. White, *America In Search of Itself* (New York: Harper & Row, Publishers, 1982), p. 108.

[50] David W. Rohde, "Committee Reform in the House of Representatives and the Subcommittee Bill of Rights," *Annals of the American Academy of Political and Social Science*, vol. 411, no. 1 (January 1974): 40, 41.

[51] President Lyndon Baines Johnson, "Remarks at the University of Michigan, May 22, 1964," Lyndon Baines Johnson Library and Museum, Austin, TX, http://www.lbjlib.utexas.edu/johnson/archives.hom/speeches.hom/640522.asp.

[52] U.S. Department of Commerce, Bureau of the Census, *Historical Statistics of the United States, Colonial Times to 1970, Part 2* (Washington, DC: GPO, 1975), pp. 1123, 1125, http://www2.census.gov/prod2/statcomp/documents/ CT1970p2-12.pdf.

[53] ACIR, *An Agenda for American Federalism: Restoring Confidence and Competence,* A-86 (Washington, DC: GPO, 1981), pp. 1-3; and James Sundquist, *Making Federalism Work* (Washington, DC: The Brookings Institution, 1969), p. 3.

[54] ACIR, *Fiscal Balance in the American Federal System, Volume 1: Basic Structure of Fiscal Federalism*, A-31 (Washington, DC: GPO, 1967), pp. 150-184.

[55] David B. Walker, *The Rebirth of Federalism: Slouching Toward Washington* (Chatham, NJ: Chatham House Publishers, Inc., 1995), pp. 70-71; and Kenneth T. Palmer, "The Evolution of Grant Policies," in *The Changing Politics of Federal Grants*, eds. Lawrence D. Brown, James W. Fossett and Kenneth T. Palmer (Washington, DC: The Brookings Institution Press, 1984), pp. 18-20.

[56] Carl W. Stenberg, "Block Grants and Devolution: A Future Tool?" in *Intergovernmental Management for the 21st Century*, eds. Timothy J. Conlan and Paul L. Posner (Washington, DC: Brookings Institution Press, 2008), p. 266.

[57] ACIR, *The Future of Federalism in the 1980s*, M-126 (Washington, DC: GPO, July 1980), p. 51.

[58] ACIR, *Categorical Grants: Their Role and Design*, A-52 (Washington, DC: GPO, 1978), p. 29.

[59] Ibid., and ACIR, *Fiscal Balance in the American Federal System, Vol. 1*, A-31 (Washington, DC: GPO, 1967), pp. 181-184.

[60] Thomas R. Dye, *Understanding Public Policy*, 6th ed. (Englewood Cliffs, NJ: Prentice-Hall, Inc., 1987), p. 301.

[61] ACIR, *Categorical Grants: Their Role and Design*, A-52 (Washington, DC: GPO, 1978), pp. 50-58; Claude E. Barfield, *Rethinking Federalism: Block Grants and Federal, State, and Local Responsibilities* (Washington, DC: American Enterprise Institute for Public Policy Research, 1981), pp. 4-8; and Thomas R. Dye, *Understanding Public Policy*, 6th ed. (Englewood Cliffs, NJ: Prentice-Hall, Inc., 1987), p. 300.

[62] Roger H. Davidson, "Representation and Congressional Committees," *The Annals of the American Academy of Political and Social Science*, vol. 411, no. 1 (January 1974), p. 50.

[63] ACIR, *Categorical Grants: Their Role and Design*, A-52 (Washington, DC: GPO, 1978), p. 65; and David Mayhew, "Congressional Elections: The Case of the Vanishing Marginals," *Polity*, vol. VI, no. 3 (Spring 1974), pp. 295-317.

[64] Claude E. Barfield, *Rethinking Federalism: Block Grants and Federal, State, and Local Responsibilities* (Washington, DC: American Enterprise Institute for Public Policy Research, 1981), p. 3.

[65] Timothy Conlan, *From New Federalism to Devolution: Twenty-Five Years of Intergovernmental Reform* (Washington, DC: The Brookings Institution, 1998), p. 62.

[66] Note: Most sources indicate that CDBG merged 7 categorical grant programs. However, one of the categorical grant programs initially designated for consolidation, the Section 312 Housing Rehabilitation Loan program, was retained as a separate program. See ACIR, *Block Grants: A Comparative Analysis*, A-60 (Washington, DC: GPO, 1977), p. 7.

[67] Carl W. Stenberg, "Block Grants and Devolution: A Future Tool?" in *Intergovernmental Management for the 21st Century*, eds. Timothy J. Conlan and Paul L. Posner (Washington, DC: Brookings Institution Press, 2008), p. 266; ACIR, *In Respect to Realities: A Report on Federalism in 1975*, M-103 (Washington, DC: GPO, April 1976), pp. 16- 20; and ACIR, *Block Grants: A Comparative Analysis*, A-60 (Washington, DC: GPO, 1977), pp. 15-40. Note: Title XX initially had all of the characteristics of a block grant and ACIR counted it as a block grant since its inception, but it was not formally called a block grant program until 1981.

[68] ACIR, *A Catalog of Federal Grant-In-Aid Programs to State and Local Governments: Grants Funded FY 1981*, M133 (Washington, DC: GPO, 1982), pp. 1-3.

[69] U.S. Office of Management and Budget, *Special Analyses: Budget of the United States Government, FY 1984* (Washington, DC: GPO, 1983), p. H-20.

[70] David B. Walker, *The Rebirth of Federalism*, 2nd ed. (New York: Chatham House Publishers, 2000), p. 127.

[71] Paul L. Posner, "Mandates: The Politics of Coercive Federalism," in *Intergovernmental Management for the 21st Century*, eds. Timothy J. Conlan and Paul L. Posner (Washington, DC: Brookings Institution Press, 2008), p. 287.

[72] 42 U.S.C. 2000d cited in ACIR, *Regulatory Federalism: Policy, Process, Impact, and Reform* (Washington, DC: GPO, 1984), p. 71.

[73] ACIR, *Regulatory Federalism: Policy, Process, Impact, and Reform* (Washington, DC: GPO, 1984), p. 71.

[74] Ibid., p. 88.

[75] Ibid., p. 246.

[76] John Kincaid, "From Cooperative to Coercive Federalism," *The Annals of the American Academy of Political and Social Science*, vol. 509, no. 1 (1990), pp. 139-152. Note: the term

coercive is often used in legal arguments to suggest that provisions of law related to federal grants-in-aid do not have constitutional standing. Federalism scholars use the term to describe, as Kincaid explained it (p. 139), the shift in emphasis "from fiscal tools to stimulate intergovernmental policy cooperation" to an increased reliance on "regulatory tools to ensure the supremacy of federal policy."

[77] David Harvey, *A Brief History of Neoliberalism* (New York: Oxford University Press, 2005); and Milton Friedman, *Free to Choose* (New York: Harcourt Brace Jovanovich, 1980).

[78] Richard L. Cole and John Kincaid, "Public Opinion and American Federalism: Perspectives on Taxes, Spending, and Trust: An ACIR Update," *Publius: The Journal of Federalism*, vol. 30, no. 1 (Winter 2000), pp. 197, 198; William G. Jacoby, "Issue Framing and Public Opinion on Government Spending," *American Journal of Political Science*, vol. 44, no. 4 (October 2000), pp. 752-758; and David B. Walker, *The Rebirth of Federalism*, 2nd ed. (New York: Chatham House Publishers, 2000), p. 341.

[79] Timothy J. Conlan and David B. Walker, "Reagan's New Federalism: Design, Debate and Discord," *Intergovernmental Perspective*, vol. 8, no. 4 (Winter 1983), pp. 6-15, 18-22.

[80] David B. Walker, Albert J. Richter, and Cynthia Colella, "The First Ten Months: Grant-In-Aid, Regulatory, and Other Changes," *Intergovernmental Perspective*, vol. 8, no. 1 (Winter 1982), pp. 5-11.

[81] U.S. General Accounting Office, *Block Grants: Characteristics, Experience and Lessons Learned*, GAO/HEHS-95- 74, February 9, 1995, p. 2, http://www.gao.gov/archive/1995/he 95074.pdf. Note: funding changes ranged from a $159 million, or 30%, reduction in the Community Services Block Grant to a $94 million, or 10%, increase in funding for the Community Development Block Grant program.

[82] ACIR, *Significant Features of Fiscal Federalism: 1985, 86 Edition* (Washington, DC: GPO, 1986), p. 19.

[83] Carl W. Stenberg, "Block Grants and Devolution: A Future Tool?" in *Intergovernmental Management for the 21st Century*, eds. Timothy J. Conlan and Paul L. Posner (Washington, DC: Brookings Institution Press, 2008), p. 267; and Timothy Conlan, *From New Federalism to Devolution: Twenty-Five Years of Intergovernmental Reform* (Washington, DC: The Brookings Institution, 1998), pp. 110-121.

[84] ACIR, *A Catalog of Federal Grant-In-Aid Programs to State and Local Governments: Grants Funded FY1984*, M139 (Washington, DC: GPO, 1984), pp. 1-3.

[85] Ibid., p. 3; Timothy Conlan, *From New Federalism to Devolution: Twenty-Five Years of Intergovernmental Reform* (Washington, DC: The Brookings Institution, 1998), p. 142; and CRS Report 87-845, *Block Grants: Inventory and Funding History*, Sandra S. Osbourn, November 21, 1986, available by request.

[86] Timothy J. Conlan and David B. Walker, "Reagan's New Federalism: Design, Debate and Discord," *Intergovernmental Perspective*, vol. 8, no. 4 (Winter 1983), p. 9. Note: The cost of the proposed trust fund was later estimated at $34.4 billion.

[87] Ibid., pp. 6-15, 18-22; and Timothy Conlan, *New Federalism: Intergovernmental Reform From Nixon to Reagan* (Washington, DC: The Brookings Institution, 1988), pp. 182-198.

[88] U.S. Office of Management and Budget, *Historical Tables: Budget of the United States Government, Fiscal Year 2009* (Washington, DC: GPO, 2008), pp. 262, 268, 276.

[89] ACIR, *Regulatory Federalism: Policy, Process, Impact, and Reform* (Washington, DC: GPO, 1984), pp. 246-249; and Timothy J. Conlan and David R. Beam, "Federal Mandates: The Record of Reform and Future Prospects," *Intergovernmental Perspective*, vol. 18, no. 4 (Fall 1992), p. 7.

[90] Timothy J. Conlan and David R. Beam, "Federal Mandates: The Record of Reform and Future Prospects," *Intergovernmental Perspective*, vol. 18, no. 4 (Fall 1992), p. 8.

[91] Ibid., p. 11.

[92] Richard P. Nathan, "The 'Devolution Revolution' An Overview," *Rockefeller Institute Bulletin* (Albany, NY: The Nelson A. Rockefeller Institute of Government, 1996), pp. 5-13; John Kincaid, "The Devolution Tortoise and the Centralization Hare," *New England Economic Review* (May/June 1998), pp. 36-38; and Chung-Lae Cho and Deil S. Wright, "The Devolution Revolution in Intergovernmental Relations in the 1990s: Changes in Cooperative and Coercive State–National Relations as Perceived by State Administrators," *Journal of Public Administration Research and Theory*, vol. 14, no. 4 (2004), pp. 447-467.

[93] For further analysis, see CRS Report R40957, *Unfunded Mandates Reform Act: History, Impact, and Issues*, by Robert Jay Dilger and Richard S. Beth.

[94] CRS Report R40957, *Unfunded Mandates Reform Act: History, Impact, and Issues*, by Robert Jay Dilger and Richard S. Beth; and U.S. Government Accountability Office, *Unfunded Mandates: Analysis of Reform Act Coverage,* GAO-04-637 (Washington, DC: GPO, 2004), p. 7.

[95] Paul Posner, "The Politics of Coercive Federalism in the Bush Era," *Publius: The Journal of Federalism*, vol. 37, no. 3 (Summer 2007), p. 403.

[96] David B. Walker, *The Rebirth of Federalism*, 2nd ed. (New York: Chatham House Publishers, 2000), p. 165.

[97] For additional analysis, see CRS Report RS22448, *Medicaid's Home and Community-Based Services State Plan Option: Section 6086 of the Deficit Reduction Act*, by Cliff Binder; and CRS Report RL31082, *Child Welfare Financing: Issues and Options*, by Karen Spar and Christine M. Devere.

[98] Richard F. Fenno, "If, as Ralph Nader Says, Congress Is "The Broken Branch," How Come We Love Our Congressmen So Much?" in *Congress in Change: Evolution and Reform*, Norman J. Ornstein, ed. (New York: Praeger Publishers, 1975), pp. 277-287.

[99] Timothy J. Conlan, "Federalism and Competing Values in the Reagan Administration," *Publius: The Journal of Federalism*, vol. 16, no. 1 (Winter 1986), p. 30.

[100] Ibid.

[101] For further analysis, see CRS Report R41105, *Fiscal Year 2011 Department of Homeland Security Assistance to States and Localities*, by Shawn Reese.

[102] Paul Posner, "The Politics of Coercive Federalism in the Bush Era," *Publius: The Journal of Federalism*, vol. 37, no. 3 (Summer 2007), pp. 397, 398; National Governors Association, "Policy Position on Secure State Driver's Licenses and Identification Cards," EC-02 (Washington, DC: National Governors Association, 2009), http://www.nga.org/portal/ site/nga/menuitem.8358ec82f5b198d18a278110501010a0/?vgnextoid= 2bdf2f9655321110VgnVCM1000001a01010aRCRD.

[103] U.S. Office of Management and Budget, *Historical Tables: Budget of the United States Government, Fiscal Year 2010* (Washington, DC: GPO, 2009), pp. 239, 282, 291; and U.S. Office of Management and Budget, *Budget of the United States Government, Fiscal Year 2013: Analytical Perspectives* (Washington, DC: GPO, 2012), p. 299.

[104] CRS computation, U.S. General Services Administration, *The Catalog of Federal Domestic Assistance* (Washington, DC: GPO, 2009), https://www.cfda.gov/downloads/ CFDA_ 2009.pdf; and U.S. General Services Administration, *The Catalog of Federal Domestic Assistance*, on-line edition, https://www.cfda.gov/.

[105] Paul Posner, "The Politics of Coercive Federalism in the Bush Era," *Publius: The Journal of Federalism*, vol. 37, no. 3 (Summer 2007), p. 399.

[106] U.S. Congressional Budget Office, *A Review of CBO's Activities in 2010 Under the Unfunded Mandates Reform Act* (Washington, DC: GPO, 2011), p. 5, http://www.cbo.gov/sites/default/files/cbofiles/ftpdocs/121xx/doc12117/03-31- umra.pdf.

[107] Ibid., pp. 292, 293. For further analysis, see CRS Report RL33960, *The Elementary and Secondary Education Act, as Amended by the No Child Left Behind Act: A Primer*, by Rebecca R. Skinner.

[108] Paul Posner, "The Politics of Coercive Federalism in the Bush Era," *Publius: The Journal of Federalism*, vol. 37, no. 3 (Summer 2007), p. 395. For further information and analysis of the Help America Vote Act, see CRS Report RL32685, *Election Reform: The Help America Vote Act and Issues for Congress*, by Eric A. Fischer and Kevin J. Coleman.

[109] U.S. Office of Management and Budget, *Analytical Perspectives: Budget of the United States Government, Fiscal Year 2011* (Washington, DC: GPO, 2010), p. 248, http://www.whitehouse.gov/sites/default/files/omb/budget/fy2011/ assets/topics.pdf.

[110] Ibid.

[111] For further analysis, see CRS Report R40223, *American Recovery and Reinvestment Act of 2009 (ARRA, P.L. 111- 5): Title V, Medicaid Provisions*, coordinated by Cliff Binder; CRS Report R40151, *Funding for Education in the American Recovery and Reinvestment Act of 2009 (P.L. 111-5)*, by Rebecca R. Skinner, David P. Smole, and Ann Lordeman; CRS Report R40214, *Transportation and Transportation Security Related Provisions of House and Senate Stimulus Legislation (H.R. 1)*, by John W. Fischer et al.; CRS Report R40211, *Human Services Provisions of the American Recovery and Reinvestment Act*, by Gene Falk et al.; CRS Report R40216, *Water Infrastructure Funding in the American Recovery and Reinvestment Act of 2009*, by Claudia Copeland, Megan Stubbs, and Charles V. Stern; CRS Report R40182, *Funding for Workforce Development in the American Recovery and Reinvestment Act (ARRA) of 2009*, by David H. Bradley and Ann Lordeman; CRS Report R40412, *Energy Provisions in the American Recovery and Reinvestment Act of 2009 (P.L. 111-5)*, coordinated by Fred Sissine; and CRS Report RS22416, *Edward Byrne Memorial Justice Assistance Grant (JAG) Program*, by Nathan James

[112] U.S. Office of Management and Budget, *Analytical Perspectives: Budget of the United States Government, Fiscal Year 2013* (Washington, DC: GPO, 2012), p. 288, http://www.whitehouse.gov/sites/default/files/omb/budget/fy2013/ assets/spec.pdf.

[113] Ibid., pp. 287, 288.

[114] ACIR's funding was withdrawn following the release for public comment and a hearing on a draft ACIR report on federal mandates. ACIR was required by UMRA to conduct the study, and to make recommendations for mitigating the effect mandates have on state and local governments. The draft report recommended the elimination of a number of federal mandates which had strong support in Congress. ACIR's commission members killed the report in a party-line vote. Many observers concluded that the draft report led to ACIR's losing its funding. See, John Kincaid, "Review of 'The Politics of Unfunded Mandates: Whither Federalism?' by Paul L. Posner," *The Academy of Political Science*, vol. 114, no. 2 (Summer 1999), pp. 322-323.

[115] U.S. Office of Management and Budget, *Budget of the United States Government, Fiscal Year 2013: Historical Tables* (Washington, DC: GPO, 2012), p. 252, http://www.whitehouse.gov/sites/default/files/omb/budget/fy2013/ assets/hist.pdf.

INDEX

#

A

B

C

D

E

F

Q

R

S

T

U

V

W

Y